# SOME ENCHANTED EVENINGS

## The Story of Rodgers and Hammerstein

### By Deems Taylor

This is the story of a revolution in the American musical theater. It was achieved by two extraordinary persons who are now introduced to their public for the first time —in the saga of entertainment history that started with Columbia Varsity Shows, through *Rose Marie* in 1924 and *The Garrick Gaieties* in 1925 to the epochal *Oklahoma!*, *South Pacific*, and all the amazing hits that continue to come from the combined genius of Richard Rodgers and Oscar Hammerstein II.

It is also the story of Lorenz Hart, the brilliant lyric writer who was the first to collaborate with Rodgers, and whose untimely death marked the end of an era in musical comedy. As Rodgers and Hart, and, later, Rodgers and Hammerstein progressed from one success to another, the careers of all three involved the theatrical greats of today and yesterday, from Mae West to Mary Martin, from Lew Fields to Ezio Pinza.

A fascinating backstage panorama, *Some Enchanted Evenings* is even more engrossing as the intimate portrait of a team which is to the present generation what Gilbert and Sullivan were to the Victorians, a team that developed in the musical play a form of art and entertainment that is uniquely American.

# Some Enchanted Evenings

*Some*

# ENCHANTED
# EVENINGS

*The story of*

## RODGERS AND
## HAMMERSTEIN

*by*

## DEEMS TAYLOR

HARPER & BROTHERS, NEW YORK

*For Linda Rodgers*
*From an elderly admirer*

Groups of illustrations follow pages
20, 68, 148 and 196

# Introduction

To write the biography of a living person is to tell an unfinished story. The sitter for your portrait doesn't hold still. By the time your book goes to press he may be dead or in jail. Or just before your book comes out he may just have published his most important work, or have invented a revolutionary device, or have been elected President of the United States.

It is even more nearly impossible to write a satisfactory biography of *two* living persons, simply because the chances of being behind the times are infinitely greater. Suppose Hammerstein should be run over by a taxicab just as this book comes out of the bindery, or should shoot Rodgers? Who would want a book as out of date as this would be? Furthermore, any proper biography should end with a profound discussion of its subject's place in history. How can I estimate the ultimate place of Rodgers and Hammerstein in the history of the American theater when they are still helping to make that history?

The best thing to do, I think, is to call this, not a biography, but a story; the story, to date, of the careers—separate and joint—of two talented people of whom I am very fond and whom I admire inordinately.

DEEMS TAYLOR

# Part One

Nobody is better qualified to write about America's most phenomenal song-writing team than Deems Taylor. For over twenty years he has been a respected and celebrated commentator on the musical scene, and is himself a composer with a number of concert and operatic hits to his credit. Mr. Taylor is known to a huge audience, through his broadcasts for the Metropolitan Opera and the New York Philharmonic, as a man of wit, erudition, and good spirits. Certainly all these qualities have gone into his account of Rodgers and Hammerstein, and will come as no surprise to readers of Mr. Taylor's other books, such as *The Well-Tempered Listener*, *Music to My Ears*, and *Of Men and Music*. As might be expected, Deems Taylor is a Doctor of Music, honorary, from five colleges—and also an honorary Doctor of Letters from another.

Mount Morris Park is a small square that sits astride New York's Fifth Avenue from 120th to 124th Streets. Today it is bounded by elderly apartments and run-down brownstone fronts. At the turn of the century, however, it was a highly desirable uptown residential district; the apartments were new, and the brownstone fronts were the homes of prosperous and solid citizens.

If you had chanced to be strolling along 120th Street some evening in, say, the year 1911, you might have heard, issuing from Number Three West, the sounds, if not of revelry by night, at least of a piano, and a reasonably adequate baritone voice rendering "Beautiful Lady" or "Tramp, Tramp, Tramp." The performers would be Dr. and Mrs. William A. Rodgers. He was a greatly respected and successful general practitioner by day, and by night, together with Mrs. Rodgers, a passionate theatergoer, with a particular preference for musical comedies.

In that respect, 1911 was especially rewarding. At the Liberty Theatre there was *The Spring Maid*, with Christie MacDonald; at the Globe, Elsie Janis in *The Slim Princess*; at the New Amsterdam, Hazel Dawn in *The Pink Lady*; at the Majestic, *The Quaker Girl*, with Ina Claire; and at the New York, Emma Trentini, a survivor of the late Manhattan Opera Company, in Victor Herbert's *Naughty*

3

*Marietta.* (The producer, prophetically enough, was Oscar Hammerstein I.)

Today, if your favorite musical comedy happens to be a hit, you can buy an album containing recordings of its entire score. But if you would like to play the music as well as hear it, you will find that, with a few exceptions (the Rodgers and Hammerstein scores are published complete), about all you can purchase will be printed copies of such five or six numbers as the publisher hopes will sell. In those days there were, of course, scant recordings and no albums. On the other hand, you could get the complete printed piano-vocal score of almost any musical comedy for a modest $2.50, take it home, and play it over to your heart's content.

Which was precisely what the Rodgers family did. Once they had attended a given musical show, the printed score would be brought home and placed on the rack of the upright piano in the second-floor living room. Thereafter, in the evenings of the ensuing two or three weeks (barring calls from patients who were tactless enough to need night visits), Mrs. Rodgers, an excellent pianist, would play, and Dr. Rodgers, looking over her shoulder, would sing. Together, they would go through the entire score, from opening chorus to finale.

Be it noted that of the five musicals mentioned, four were the work of British or Continental composers. Even Herbert, the fifth, who was technically an American, was Viennese in style. We were still in the thrall of the craze for transatlantic operettas, a craze that had begun with Henry W. Savage's production of *The Merry Widow* in

1907. In 1911, Rudolf Friml and Jerome Kern had a year to wait before seeing their first Broadway productions, *Firefly* and *The Red Petticoat*; and not until 1913 was Sigmund Romberg to see *his* first, *The Midnight Girl*.

One faithful listener at these 1911 *soirées musicales* would undoubtedly be the youngest member of the family, nine-year-old Richard Rodgers. Born on June 28, 1902, he had been exposed, so to speak, to the family concerts since infancy. By age four, as the insurance agents word it, he could be found at the piano, pecking out tentative one-finger versions of the songs he had heard. By the time he was six he had taught himself to play with both hands—and, as he modestly admits, pretty well at that.

The average small boy tends to entertain not so much one life's ambition as a series of them—a yearning, for example, to be successively a fireman, a major general, a cowboy, President of the United States, and an all-American fullback. Dick Rodgers cannot remember a time when he did not want to be a musician. As he puts it: "What I am doing today is what I have wanted to do all my life." At ten, he was making up tunes and playing them. At twelve, he was at the piano for as many hours as attendance at Public School 166 would allow. In the summer of 1916 he attended a boys' camp in Maine, where the fourteen-year-old maestro composed his first, genuine words-and-music song. It was called—you'd never guess—"Campfire Days." It is rumored that about that same time he wrote another, much more sophisticated ditty, "My Auto Show Girl." Incidentally, these are two of the comparatively few songs that he ever wrote that were not composed specifically for the stage. The theater is his first and last love—any theater; not necessarily musical shows alone. He would save up his weekly allowance and squander it all on Saturday matinees. "My week began," he says, "at two-thirty on Saturday and ended at five-fifteen."

The year 1917 saw his first important achievement, when he composed the complete score for an amateur musical comedy given by a boys' athletic club in aid of the New York *Sun*'s cigarette fund for American soldiers in France. The performance took place in the grand ballroom of the Hotel Plaza, before a presumably brilliant audience. The proud composer conducted the five-piece orchestra.

Having undergone his baptism of fire, and tasted blood —which is admittedly a pretty rickety metaphor, but does cover the ground—he left no room for any doubts as to his vocation. Every minute that De Witt Clinton High School left free was devoted to making up tunes, tunes, all kinds of tunes and (he had picked up notation somehow) writing them down. However, one frustrating fact presented itself. "Songs Without Words" may be all right for Mendelssohn, but they are not of much avail for one who wishes to write for the theater. He needed lyrics. He tried his hand at some of his own, and even nagged his brother and his father into trying *their* hands. But the family output left something to be desired.

As if on cue, in walked the god from the machine in the person of one Philip Leavitt, a gentleman in the paint business who was a friend of Richard's elder brother, Mortimer. Like most visitors to the Rodgers ménage, he had heard many of the budding composer's tunes, and liked them. He was, consequently, keenly conscious of the dilemma in which Dick found himself: of having nobody to write words to his music. Something must be done about that. Accordingly, one Sunday afternoon in 1918 he called for Richard, took him uptown in the subway (the family had moved to 161 West Eighty-sixth Street in 1911), and marched him up the front steps of another brownstone front in 119th Street, only a block south of the former Rodgers home. There he introduced him to a friend of his named Lorenz Hart. Young Hart's trouble was Richard's in reverse. He had words, but no music.

In its own small way the meeting was as momentous as that of Tristan and Isolde or Anthony and Cleopatra. Hart showed Rodgers some of his lyrics, and Rodgers played Hart some of his tunes. Instantly they realized that each needed the other. That Sunday afternoon saw the beginning of a partnership that endured until Hart's death, over a quarter of a century later.

The new team moved into action at once, with abounding enthusiasm and grim determination. They tried songs on publishers, only to encounter the age-old question that publishers always ask of unknowns: "Who's going to sing it?" They tried producers, and were invited to go get a reputation. Foiled in this direction, they took to writing amateur shows—book, lyrics, and music—which were performed by various groups at benefits.

All this activity was giving them experience, true enough, but it wasn't getting them any nearer to Broadway. Just at the right time help came, in the form, once more, of the never-sufficiently-to-be-thanked Philip Leavitt. He had been following their activities with unflagging interest (doubtless much to the detriment of the paint business), and had been impressed, not only with the quality of their work together, but also with their persistence in trying to get it produced. Once again he decided that something had to be done, and once again he did it.

For thirty years, from 1885 to 1915, the fabulous German-dialect team of Weber and Fields had been an American institution. Their outrageous puns, mangled English, *non sequiturs*, and general inspired idiocy made them the darlings of vaudeville and their own revues—if one could apply that term to the rowdy goings-on at their music hall. The famous drugstore scene, which began—

WEBER: I vant some talcum powder.
FIELDS: Mennens?
WEBER: No, vimmens.
FIELDS: You vant it scented?
WEBER: No, I take it home myself.

—or the episode in which Fields, deciding to commit suicide, went offstage brandishing a revolver, fired a shot, and returned, caroling, "Missed!"—nonsense such as that laid 'em in the aisles at the turn of the century.[1]

When the long partnership was finally dissolved, Lew Fields branched out as a producer of musical comedies, some of which he wrote, and in most of which he starred. It was to Fields's home in Far Rockaway, on another Sunday afternoon, that Leavitt took sixteen-year-old Rodgers. There the boy met, not only Fields, but his son Herbert (who

[1] It still does. That joke is now current on television.

was destined to write the book of many a Rodgers and Hart show) and his young daughter Dorothy. He spent the afternoon playing over his songs for the famous producer. Then the miracle happened. It would have been easy for Fields to have given him a figurative pat on the head with something such as, "You've got some nice things there. Keep it up. You boys will make it yet." Instead, he announced that he liked one of the songs, "Any Old Place with You," so much that he was going to find a spot for it in *A Lonely Romeo*, a show of his that was currently running at the Casino Theatre.

He kept his word. "Any Old Place with You" went into the show, sung by Eve Lynn and Alan Hale, and stayed there. Rodgers and Hart were professionals. They had a song on Broadway, and a real, live publisher was printing it.

You will find it as the first offering in *The Rodgers and Hart Song Book*. It is an interesting exhibit, not only because one of its authors was a sixteen-year-old high school senior, but also for certain unconventionalities that now seem significant. For one thing, it has a thirty-two-bar verse and a sixteen-bar chorus, a complete reversal of what was common practice among song writers in those days. The opening measures of the chorus do bear a certain faint, family resemblance to that classic of the gay nineties, "Ta-ra-ra BOOM-dee-yay," but it possesses certain features, such as the free use of secondary seventh chords and suspensions upward (to be nastily technical about it), that are characteristic of the later Rodgers. The lyric abounds in the unexpected rhymes, such as—

In dreamy Portugal
I'm goin' to court you, gal,

or

I'd go to hell for ya
Or Philadelphia

—that are unmistakably Hart.

In the fall of 1919, at the age of seventeen, young Rodgers matriculated at Columbia University. I once asked him, "Why Columbia, rather than any other college?" His reply was simplicity itself: "The varsity show."

Pressed for details, he elaborated.

"Yes, the varsity show. It used to run every year for a week in the Hotel Astor ballroom, with a professional orchestra. I intended to write it. What better incentive could you have for going to college? Columbia was obviously the only place to go."

Queried as to his academic courses, he was equally brief and to the point: "Whatever books I didn't have to open."

However languid he may have been regarding his intramural duties, he showed no lack of diligence in the pursuit of his main objective. Luckily for the team, Hart, as an alumnus, was eligible to work on a varsity show. The two produced the lyrics and music, and Hart collaborated with the faithful Philip Leavitt on a book that they adapted from a story by Milton Kroops, another alumnus. The finished produce was duly submitted to the show committee, and was as duly accepted. One of the judges was an alumnus and fraternity brother of Dick's, Oscar Hammerstein II, who had not only written a varsity show but had acted in one. They had met five years before, when Hammerstein was a nineteen-year-old junior and Rodgers an awestruck youngster of twelve. "It was like meeting Eisenhower," he reports.

The first complete Rodgers and Hart show, *Fly With Me*, was produced in the grand ballroom of the Hotel Astor for a week in the spring of 1920. The orchestra, augmented to twenty-four pieces, was conducted by the composer. Incidentally, it was the first varsity show ever to have been composed by a freshman. As if all this were not enough glory, Lew Fields attended one performance of *Fly With Me* and promptly acquired the lyrics and the music, which he put into a musical comedy, *The Poor Little Ritz Girl*, written by one George Campbell and himself.

History does not record whether Mr. Fields was playing safe, or whether there were not enough numbers in the original score, but when, after a late spring tryout in Boston, the show opened at the Central Theatre on Wednesday, July 28, 1920, our boys shared the lyrics and music with Sigmund Romberg and Alex Gerber. Rodgers and Hart had seven numbers, Romberg and Gerber, eight.

It is to be assumed that on the day after the opening the newly fledged authors bought all the papers, to see what the critics had to say. If they did, they found what are known as "mixed" notices. The New York *Sun* and *Herald* announced that "there was a waltz movement in Mr. Romberg's familiar and Viennese manner that was worth the rest of the music together." On the other hand, according to Heywood Broun, of the *Tribune*, "The neglected lyric also gets more of its due than usual, for the song entitled

'Mary, Queen of Scots' seems to us the most rollicking ballad we have heard in a twelvemonth. The more serious and sentimental numbers are from Sigmund Romberg, and they are pleasing, but hardly as striking as the lighter numbers."

There was a slight difference of opinion regarding the book, also, which the *World* announced as having "a real plot, humor, a good-looking chorus, and a tuneful score. The musical numbers are never allowed to interfere with the progress of the plot"—whereas the *Evening Sun* declared that there was "a plot that makes an occasional appearance when costumes and tenors are getting ready to appear." The end of July is a perilous time for any musical to be opening. Nevertheless, despite the unseasonable date, *The Poor Little Ritz Girl* lasted until November, closing after a respectable run of 119 performances.

It had been an eventful year—a varsity show produced and then bought for Broadway. Then came a lull. In Dick's sophomore year he and Larry Hart wrote another varsity show, *You'll Never Know*, which was duly produced at the Astor with the composer conducting. But if Lew Fields attended, he gave no sign. *We'll* never know what that show was like.

At the end of his sophomore year, Dick, with the blessings of his family, left Columbia to enroll for a two-year course at the Institute of Musical Art (now the Juilliard School of Music), where he took lecture courses and studied harmony and ear training. During the Institute years he managed to maintain his contact with the theater in a highly practical manner.

In 1921 the Messrs. Shubert were occupied in building a vaudeville chain in opposition to the Keith-Albee circuit, which dominated the vaudeville field much as Klaw and Erlanger had dominated the "legitimate" theater in former years. In pursuit of their campaign they organized what were known as "Shubert Units," which they sent on the road. Every unit was a complete show, the first half being a series of vaudeville acts, the second, a tabloid musical comedy. Young Rodgers, obtaining a leave of absence from the Institute, spent a season on the road, conducting one of the tabloids. It was a valuable experience. The conductor of a musical show is not only in constant touch with the actors, but is more or less responsible for holding the show together, besides being in an ideal position to sense the reactions of the audience.

Meanwhile, Rodgers and Hart were not neglecting their studies together. Not long ago, Dick gave this as his recipe for success in the musical theater:

1. Be in the center of things, i.e., live in New York, where almost all of the musical shows originate.

2. Want what you want more than anything else in the world.

3. Work at it constantly.

To which might be added, "Be as talented as Rodgers and Hart." Taking the last for granted, the formula is a good one, and the two were faithfully adhering to it even in the early 1920's. Since the professional producers took a resolutely dim view of the fruits of their labors, they pursued the nonprofessionals. They went back to writing a series of amateur shows, which were performed in fundraising campaigns of various sorts, in churches, synagogues, girls' schools, boys' schools—any cause or auditorium that would give them a production.

The next break came, again, from Lew Fields. In addition to their lyrical creations, the two had collaborated with Herbert Fields in a three-act comedy called *The Melody Man*. It concerned the struggles of an elderly Austrian composer to write his own music, instead of arranging jazz songs. Two Rodgers and Hart numbers, "Moonlight Mama" and "I'd Like to Poison Ivy," were embedded in the plot, as burlesque examples of "pop" song writing. The authorship of the piece was credited to Herbert Richard Lorenz, a pseudonym that should not be too difficult for you to penetrate. Lew Fields produced it at the Ritz Theatre on May 13, 1924, playing the title role himself in a cast that included an unknown juvenile named Fredric March.

According to Alexander Woollcott, in the *Sun*, the play had "some enormously comic interludes." Quinn Martin, in the *World*, called it "one of the surprises of this dramatic season. It is a tremendously funny show." Not so Percy Hammond, in the *Herald Tribune*, who pronounced it "feeble, immature, and meandering," while John Corbin of the *Times*, remarked that "the only question with regard to it is just how easy it is to amuse those who are easily amused." The unkindly verdict of Hammond and Corbin seems to have been decisive, for *The Melody Man* closed after a few performances. Once more Rodgers and Hart had reached a dead end. Once more they went back to the amateur field.

All during those years Dr. William Rodgers had been

behaving in a highly unorthodox manner. Given a physician who has two sons, one of whom wants to follow his father's profession, while the other, younger son wants to be a composer, his traditional reaction, by all the rules of sound fiction, would be to encourage the would-be physician and urge the would-be composer to take up some honest line of business. Dr. Rodgers did just the opposite. He tried to discourage the elder son, Mortimer, from studying medicine, on the grounds that doctoring was a dog's life (Dr. Mortimer Rodgers is today one of the country's leading obstetricians), and did everything he could to further the ambitions of the young composer.

Even so, by the spring of 1925 the spirits and fortunes of the partners had reached an all-time low. Producers were unwilling even to look at their work, let alone consider producing it. Hart had made some money translating a couple of Viennese operettas for the Shuberts. This capital he had invested in two productions of his own, which had opened and closed with dizzying rapidity. Rodgers' father paid his bills, and was apparently willing to do so indefinitely. But if Rodgers *père* didn't mind, Rodgers *fils* did. He was tired of being a burden. He was twenty-three years old, had been knocking on the door of the theater for five years, and had yet to earn his keep. Besides, he was in debt. His allowance sufficed for necessities, but was insufficient to finance his lighter moments. He had got into the habit of borrowing five dollars from a friend every time he went dancing. The debt now amounted to $105. The friend, instead of pressing him for payment, took a much more practical step. He obtained for young Rodgers the offer of a job, at fifty dollars a week, selling what was euphemistically called "babies' underwear."

It is interesting, if not significant, that Rodgers and Hart received their first practical encouragement at the hands of two laymen. The first was Philip Leavitt, who arranged the meeting of the two and the audition for Lew Fields. The second was a theatrical lawyer named Benjamin Kaye, a patient of Dr. Rodgers and an admirer of the Rodgers and Hart songs. One Sunday night in the early spring of 1925 he telephoned Richard. Would he and Larry Hart care to write the songs for an intimate revue that a group of talented young people were putting together? Richard would not. Thanks just the same, but he and Larry just weren't interested in doing any more amateur shows. Besides, he had a job, and was starting to work the following morning.

"That's too bad," observed Mr. Kaye. "The Theatre Guild will be disappointed."

"THE THEATRE GUILD??" remarked Richard, in tones that rocked Eighty-sixth Street to its foundations.

Mr. Kaye explained. The Guild, having floated a bond issue and built the new Guild Theatre, was contemplating buying two large tapestries to be draped from the boxes. To raise the money for these, the directors had decided to let a group of extras and understudies put on a small revue. He, Kaye, had suggested Rodgers and Hart for the score, and the Guild had agreed.

Next morning the babies missed their underwear. Rodgers and Hart were at work.

Alfred Lunt and Lynn Fontanne were nearing the end

of a run in Molnar's *The Guardsman* at the Guild's Garrick Theatre. And it was in that theater, on Sunday afternoon and evening, May 17, 1925, that the little revue, christened *The Garrick Gaieties*, played what were supposed to be its only two performances. The program comprised twenty-three numbers—songs, sketches, and dances. The authors included Benjamin Kaye, Newman Levy, Sam Jaffe, and Morrie Ryskind. Carolyn Hancock (who was also Mrs. Lee Simonson) had designed most of the sets and costumes, the remainder having been contributed by Miguel Covarrubias. Herbert Fields had staged the dances. The cast, most of whom nobody had ever heard of up to then, included Sterling Holloway, Edith Meiser, Lee Strasberg, Betty Starbuck, June Cochrane, House Jameson, Philip Loeb, and Romney Brent. The show was budgeted at three thousand dollars (Mr. Rodgers has recently confided that *The King and I* cost a little more than one hundred times that sum).

The *Gaieties*, being a benefit, was technically not subject to criticism. Nevertheless, although the Guild, beyond contributing the theater, ostentatiously kept hands off the production (Philip Loeb was the producer of record), such was the prestige of the Guild name that most of the first-string dramatic critics attended the opening. What they found was something that had wit, taste, a fresh point of view, and lovely tunes, something more engaging than the humorless lavishness of *Artists and Models* and the Ziegfeld *Follies*. The Monday morning reports were raves.

"Fresh and spirited and engaging . . . bright with the brightness of something new minted," wrote Woollcott in

17

the *Sun.* Gilbert Gabriel of the *Telegram-Mail* reported it as "a witty, boisterous, athletic chow-chow. . . . The music by Richard Rodgers is fitting and enlivening." The *Graphic* announced that it had "some lovely ensemble numbers with hit music which would be used in any Broadway review." According to the News, "The music, by Richard Rodgers, and the lyrics, by Lorenz Hart . . . were well above the average Broadway product." The *American* said that it "went over like a bunch of firecrackers," a sentiment that was echoed by the *Telegraph* and the *Mirror. Variety,* the hardheaded bible of show business, pronounced the ulti-mate verdict: "A corking revue . . . Rodgers and Hart's stuff clicked here like a colonel's heels at attention."

After such breath-taking unanimity of opinion there was nothing to do but announce two more performances on the following Sunday. These were sold out by Wednes-day. Whereupon Dick Rodgers sought out Theresa Hel-burn, the executive director of the Theatre Guild.

"Why," he wanted to know, "don't you put *The Gar-rick Gaieties* on for a regular Broadway run?"

"Where?" she asked.

"At the Garrick, of course."

"And just what do we do with *The Guardsman?*"

"Close it."

The calm effrontery of this suggestion caused her to totter slightly. When she could speak again she had an amended suggestion.

"Suppose we do this," she said. "Suppose we run the *Gaieties* for four afternoons on the days when *The Guards-man* has no matinees—that is, Monday, Tuesday, Wednes-

*18*

day, and Friday—and see how well it does. If it goes really well, I'll close *The Guardsman.*"

This was done. *The Garrick Gaieties* gave four matinee performances during the week of June 1, 1925—the hottest week of that year. The crowds literally mobbed the theater, and there were standees at every performance. Miss Helburn kept her word. *The Guardsman* closed on Saturday night, June 6, 1925 (to the secret relief of Lunt and Fontanne, who wanted to go home), and on the following Monday the *Gaieties* settled down to a twenty-five-week run that ended on November 28, after 161 performances. Rodgers and Hart were "in." Literally overnight they had been taken out of the ranks of the struggling unknowns to be a team that commanded the respectful consideration of any producer of musical shows.

Their next production was one to evoke memories of Raymond Hitchcock's famous ditty, "Ain't It Funny What a Diff'rence Just a Few Hours Make?"—except that in this case it should read "months." Shortly after the production of the ill-fated *The Melody Man* Rodgers and Hart, together with Herbert Fields, had written a piece based on an alleged incident of the American Revolution, wherein a certain Mrs. Robert Murray, a New Yorker, had artfully detained the staff of General Howe's army of occupation by inviting them to dinner, thereby giving General George Washington time in which to withdraw his Colonial troops to more tenable positions.

This opus they had peddled industriously for nearly a year, with spectacular nonsuccess. Aside from the fact that the three were virtually unknown, other reasons why they failed to sell their brain child were, probably, because it was a "costume piece," and its setting wasn't romantic. Now costume pieces were all very well—there was, in fact, a great demand for them—provided their locale was some distant country. The successful musical comedies of the period, shows such as *The Vagabond King, The Student Prince, Rose Marie, Princess Flavia,* had one thing in common: their setting was anywhere but America. Here was a piece whose action not only took place in unromantic New York, but was concerned with—of all things—American history. Small wonder that the producers looked the other way.

The *Gaieties* changed all that. A little over three months after it (or is it "they"?) opened—September 18, 1925, to be exact—George Ford presented *Dearest Enemy* at the Knickerbocker Theatre, with the composer conducting. Flavia Arcaro, as Mrs. Murray, supplied the intrigue, with Helen Ford contributing the love interest. The critics were kind. Percy Hammond, in the *Herald Tribune,* called it "a baby grand opera . . . polite, sentimental, and prettily embroidered." The *Times* said that "it blooms with a fresh charm," and that it offered "compositions of genuine musical quality." The *Telegram* announced, "Rodgers continues to improve markedly with every score"—not a very lengthy continuity, considering that this was Rodgers' second full-length offering. Best of all, the theatergoers took it to their collective bosom from the start. The show ran for nine months, closing in May, 1926.

While I am not absolutely certain, I am pretty sure that 1926 established some sort of record. For that was the year

Richard Rodgers. (Photo by Philip Shultz)

Richard Rodgers at the piano while Lorenz Hart looks on. Together they wrote the music and lyrics to twenty-seven shows. (Culver Service.)

# The Wigwam

## 1916

### Music to "Camp-Fire Days"

#### By Richard Rodgers

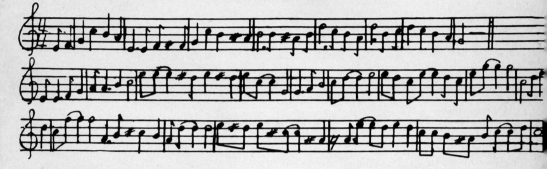

### CAMP-FIRE DAYS.

When the pine-bough flames on high,
When big Bear Lake drinks down the sky,
We'll gather round, with tuneful sound,
Some red-hot corn to try.

### Pierre Patelin

#### A Fifteenth Century Farce
#### From the French

##### By Maurice Relonde

Above, Rodgers' first composition, written at the age of fourteen. Below, right, Lew Fields, with whose help Rodgers and Hart first became professionals. (Culver Service.) In May of 1924 he presented and played in *The Melody Man* by Herbert Richard Lorenz, a pseudonym for Herbert Fields, Rodgers and Hart.

BEGINNING TUESDAY EVENING, MAY 13, 1924
Matinees Wednesday and Saturday

## LEW FIELDS
— in —

## "THE MELODY MAN"

A Three-Act Comedy
By Herbert Richard Lorenz
Staged by Lawrence Marston and Alexander Leftwich

### Cast of Characters
(In Order of Appearance)

| | |
|---|---|
| JESSIE SANDS, the telephone girl | ELEANOR ROWE |
| SIDNEY, office boy | JERRY DEVINE |

| | | |
|---|---|---|
| THE SAXOPHONE | | FRED STARWER |
| THE CORNET | | JOE LINDWURM |
| THE TROMBONE | Jos. B. Franklin's Revellers | DAVE STRYKER |
| THE PIANO | | AL SCHENCK |
| THE DRUMS | | BILL TUCKER |

RUTH DAVIS, a small time ballad singer......LOUISE KELLEY
STELLA MALLORY, professional manager of the
  Al. Tyler Music Pub. Co....................EVA PUCK
DONALD CLEMENS, a student violinist.......FREDRIC MARCH
Al. Tyler Music Pub. Co..............DONALD GALLAHER
BERT HACKETT and ⎱A Married Vaudeville Team ⎰SAM WHITE
RITA LA MARR..⎰ ⎱RENEE NOEL
ELSA HENKEL, his secretary..............BETTY WESTON
DONALD CLEMENS, a student violinist......FREDRIC MARCH
FRANZ HENKEL, arranger of music with the company,
                              LEW FIELDS
DAVE LOEB, a police court lawyer..........JULES JORDAN
A CHAUFFEUR..........................JOSEPH TORPEY
A MAID.............................SARA CHAPELLE
A PIANO PLAYER with the company..........JIMMY KAPFER

Here are three members of the cast of *The Poor Little Ritz Girl*, Grant Simpson, Lulu McConnell and Aileen Poe. (Culver Service.)

# Week of May 24, 1920

**Evenings at 8.15**
**Matinees Wednesday and Saturday at 2.15**

Mr. Lew Fields Presents

## "The Poor Little Ritz Girl"

**An Original Musical Comedy in Two Acts and Four Scenes**

**Book by Henry B. Stillman**

**Music by Richard C. Rodgers**

**Lyrics by Lorenz M. Hart**

**Book by Wm. J. O'Neil**

**Musical Numbers and Ensembles arranged by David Bennett**

**The Entire Production Devised and Staged under the Personal Supervision of Mr. Lew Fields**

*The Poor Little Ritz Girl* opened in New York in July, 1920, and ran for 119 performances. Here is the program for the Boston try-out.

On May 17, 1925, *The Garrick Gaieties*, a Theatre Guild production opened and over-night Rodgers and Hart were "in." The picture shows the chorus from a musical num-ber called "April Fool." (Culver Service.)

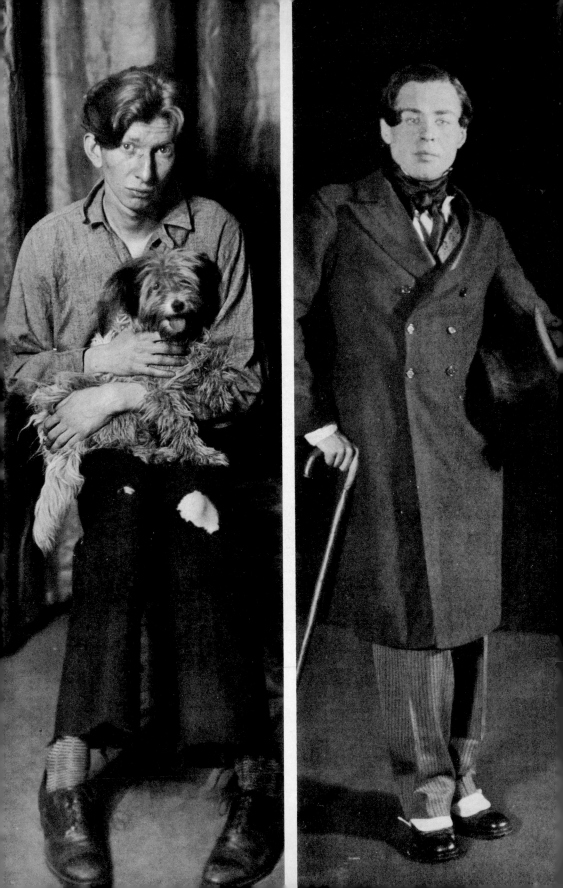

In September, 1925, George Ford presented *Dearest Enemy*, a romantic costume musical that ran for 286 performances. Based on an alleged incident of the American Revolution with the action taking place in New York, it was a departure from the current tradition of setting costumed romances in a distant locale. (Courtesy of Rodgers and Hammerstein.)

Sterling Holloway, left, and Romney Brent, right, were two of the featured players in the first and second *Garrick Gaieties*. (Courtesy of The Theatre Guild.)

*Girl Friend*, which opened at the Vanderbilt Theater in March of 1926, was another Lew Fields production with a contemporary setting and a story based on the contemporary craze of six-day bicycle racing. The show had a run of 103 performances and left behind two lasting hits, "Blue Room" and the title song. (Culver Service.)

Bea Lillie, in a wonderful costume, starred in *She's My Baby*, which opened at the Globe in January, 1927. (Culver Service.)

William Gaxton and Constance Carpenter in a romantic pose from the *Connecticut Yankee,* among the best known of all Rodgers and Hart shows. William Gaxton played the Yankee and Constance Carpenter the Demoiselle Alisande le Carteloise, and together they sang "My Heart Stood Still" and "Thou Swell." The show opened at the Vanderbilt Theatre in November, 1927, and ran for 266 performances. (Culver Service.)

*Present Arms,* produced by Lew Fields in 1928, had a run of 155 performances and left behind the all-time favorite song "You Took Advantage of Me." The Marine is Fuller Mellish, Jr., the girl Demaris Dore. (Culver Service.)

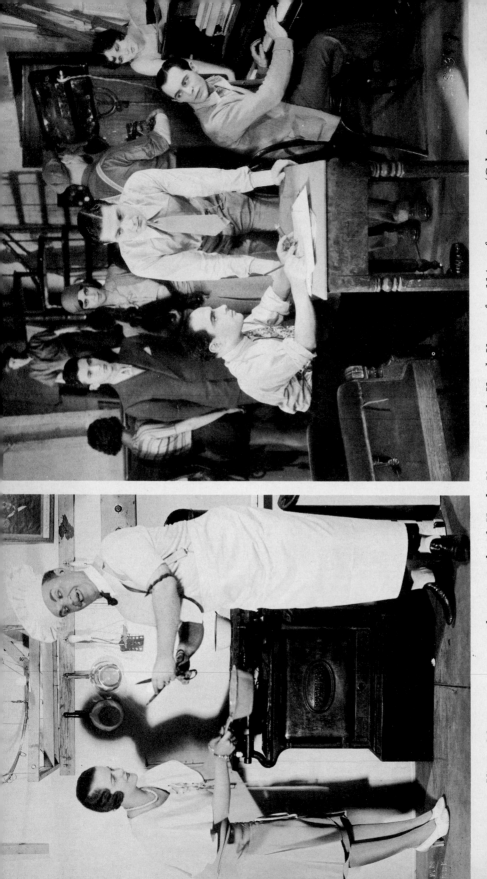

Victor Moore was among the principals of *Heads Up,* which opened at the Alvin Theatre on November 11, 1929, thirteen days after the stock-market crash. Despite the crash, *Heads Up* ran for 114 performances. (Culver Service.) Composer Rodgers at the piano and lyrist Hart seated at the table are seen rehearsing on stage. (Culver Service.)

*Simple Simon*, starring Ed Wynn, opened at the Ziegfeld in February, 1930. Above is première danseuse Harriet Hoctor in the "Hunting Ballet." (Culver Service.) Below, Richard Rodgers with Maurice Chevalier, who starred in the Rodgers and Hart movie musical *Love Me Tonight*. (Courtesy of Rodgers and Hammerstein.)

The New York première of the movie *Hallelujah, I'm a Bum* took place in February, 1933. This picture, taken in 1932, shows Al Jolson rehearsing with Rodgers standing behind him. In this picture Rodgers and Hart experimented with "rhythmic dialogue," a method of writing most of the dialogue in rhyme and having it sung.

*Jumbo*, presented by Billy Rose, opened in November, 1935, at the New York Hippodrome. The nine-month run marked a successful return to Broadway for Rodgers and Hart after their Hollywood absence. (Courtesy of Rodgers and Hammerstein.)

*I'd Rather Be Right*, a political satire, opened at the Alvin in 1937. George M. Cohan played the part of the President of the United States, who struggles in vain to balance the budget. (Culver Service.)

in which the boys lost their heads completely and turned out five shows, four of which were produced in New York and one in London. Obviously they did not lack for producers. As a matter of fact, after the *Gaieties* they never did lack for producers. Their entire career, barring one three-year period which we shall discuss later, was a continuous success story. In those brave days any musical comedy that ran a hundred performances, roughly three months, could "get off the nut"—that is, pay back its original investment. Most of the Rodgers and Hart offerings did much better than that. In fact, of the twenty-seven shows that they wrote together, only three can be counted as failures.

The first of the 1926 crop, *The Girl Friend,* opened at the Vanderbilt Theatre on St. Patrick's Day, with Lew Fields as the producer. Its story, as unfolded by Herbert Fields, was that of a young Long Island dairy farmer and his ambition to become a great six-day bicycle rider—an ambition shared by his trainer-manager-press agent girl friend. The papers, on the whole, were pleased: "As dainty and sprightly as anything the season has managed to put together" . . . "lilting tunes aplenty, good dancing, comedy" . . . "this WAS music, instead of molasses." Only the *Evening World* (Bide Dudley) found it "a so-so lightweight musical comedy."

One characteristic of the Rodgers and Hart shows is that virtually every one contributed at least one song that has long outlived its original setting. *The Garrick Gaieties*, for example, contributed two such: "Sentimental Me" and the delectable "Manhattan." *Dearest Enemy* brought forth

"Here in My Arms." *The Girl Friend* gave us two more: the title song and "Blue Room." The G.F. ran for 103 performances. Meanwhile, there was more, much more, to come.

The second production of that fabulous '26 was the second edition of *The Garrick Gaieties,* which opened on May 10. This time the Theatre Guild abandoned its attitude of indulgent aloofness and emerged as the producer. Nor was this a benefit, to raise money for tapestries. It was a Guild Production. About a third of the cast was made up of veterans of the first *Gaieties,* and some of the original authors contributed new material. All together, there were twenty-one sketches and songs. The critics were less surprised, but equally hospitable. Brooks Atkinson pronounced it "the most intelligent revue in town." According to Alexander Woollcott, "A nervous and tentative experiment a year ago, it is already an accepted institution in the life of our town." Burns Mantle opined that "the score is pretty sure to be one of the most popular of the summer." And so it was. Also, true to form, it bequeathed at least one number to posterity, "Mountain Greenery," still one of the most popular of the Rodgers and Hart songs.

The show ran for 174 performances, thirteen more than the first *Gaieties.* Also, it established another record, unbeaten, I believe, even by the prolific Victor Herbert. Rodgers and Hart now had three shows running on Broadway (a feat that Rodgers was to duplicate twenty-six years later): the *Gaieties* at the Garrick, *Dearest Enemy* at the Knickerbocker, and *The Girl Friend* at the Vanderbilt. Just what the author's weekly aggregate royalties amounted to, history does not relate; however, one would probably be safe in calling them a living wage (bearing in mind that the Federal income tax was a crushing 4 per cent). In any case, Rodgers remained calm, his only extravagance being a La Salle coupe with a bright crimson body and a black top.

Meanwhile, the fame of this successful new team had spread to England, where the actor-producer Jack Hurlbert had invited the two to come over and write lyrics and music for a new musical comedy. This they did, working through the summer. Early in September, when the new show was ready for rehearsal, they hurried back to the States to work on two fresh New York productions.

On December 1, 1926, Hurlbert produced *Lido Lady* at the Gaiety Theatre in London. It was an all-American attraction. Besides introducing Rodgers and Hart to the British public it had a book by Guy Bolton, Bert Kalmar, and Harry Ruby. The score contained six brand-new songs, a seventh, new to England at least, being our valued friend, "Here in My Arms." The critics were cordial. The London *Era* called it "a brilliant production, full of witty lines and good comedy business . . . delightfully jolly music." The *Stage* found it "a most successful production," with which the *Queen* wholeheartedly agreed.

A little over three weeks later, on December 27, at the Vanderbilt Theatre, Lew Fields and Lyle D. Andrews presented the fifth Rodgers and Hart show of 1926, *Peggy Ann*. Herbert Fields wrote the book, based on Edgar Smith's *Tillie's Nightmare* which Marie Dressler had played in New York about twelve years before. *Peggy Ann* broke all the rules. Most of it was the story of a dream, in which boy met girl under far from romantic circumstances. There was no opening chorus, and the finale was played in the dark. Moreover, four other shows opened that same night, and it was several days before the first-string critics got around to seeing it. But by the time they did get around, *Peggy Ann* was already a hit. Helen Ford acted and sang the title role, ably abetted by Lulu Mc-Connell, who in recent years has won acclaim for her inspired lunacy in the broadcast, "It Pays to Be Ignorant." Two of the songs, "A Tree in the Park" and "Where's That Rainbow?" are still with us.

The last Rodgers and Hart venture for 1926 was *Betsy* —which might have been subtitled, "Oops! Sorry." Florenz Ziegfeld produced it at the New Amsterdam Theatre on December 28, the evening after the opening of *Peggy Ann*. The book, concerned with a young lady's yearnings to find a husband, had been sired by Irving Caesar and David Freedman, and revised by Anthony Maguire. But despite the efforts of three authors and Belle Baker, who played the title role, *Betsy* received a cool reception. The critics took a dim view of the whole proceedings, one or two even casting a slight scowl in the direction of Rodgers and Hart. *Betsy* went the way of all flesh after thirty-nine performances, leaving behind only one memorable song, Irving Berlin's "Blue Skies," which had been interpolated in the score for Miss Baker.

No sooner was *Peggy Ann* tucked away and *Betsy* laid to rest than the two returned to London, inspired by a pardonable curiosity as to what *Lido Lady* looked and sounded like. In the course of their inspection tour they met the great C. B. Cochran, who pointed out that as long as they were in London they might as well provide the score for a new revue that he was in the process of constructing. Having a few weeks to spare, they agreed.

In due time—May 20, 1927, to be exact—the new opus, tersely entitled *One Dam Thing After Another*, with a score by Rodgers and Hart, opened at the London Pavilion, where it was destined to run for the balance of the year. The smash hit of the show was a song, "My Heart Stood Still"—of which, more later. To call the story of its origin a twice-told tale would be a gross understatement. It has appeared in print several times, and Mr. Rodgers, for one, moans softly and leaves the room whenever it is mentioned. Nevertheless, for the benefit of the handful of persons who may not have heard it, here it is, once more.

The setting was a taxi, in which Rodgers and Hart and two feminine acquaintances were rounding the Place de la Concorde (just what they were doing in Paris, when they were supposed to be hard at work in London, has never been explained). Another taxi, driven by the customary Parisian homicidal maniac, swept past them at breakneck speed, missing a disastrous sideswipe by exactly three-sixteenths of an inch (9.4 millimeters). When the four passengers had regained the power of speech one of the girls murmured, "Oh-h! My heart stood still!"

"That," remarked Master Hart, "would be a hell of a good title for a song."

No more was said at the moment; but a couple of weeks later Rodgers approached his partner with a manuscript.

"Here's a tune for that title of yours."

"What title?"

" 'My Heart Stood Still.' "

The rest, of course, is anything but silence.

The show with which "My Heart Stood Still" is associated—*A Connecticut Yankee*—was six years in getting on the boards. Some time in 1921, during the run of *The Poor Little Ritz Girl*, Herbert Fields saw Harry C. Myers in a silent motion picture version of *A Connecticut Yankee in King Arthur's Court*, and decided that it would make a wonderful musical comedy. He confided this idea to Rodgers and Hart, who saw the picture and enthusiastically agreed. How were they to know that four years must elapse before any songs of theirs would be heard on Broadway? They had a musical show running, didn't they? And it was a hit, wasn't it? And wasn't it reasonable to assume that at any moment the producers would be beating a path to the Rodgers and Hart door? The answer to these academic questions being yes, Rodgers obtained from the Mark Twain estate a six-months' option on the musical comedy rights to *The Yankee*. But the producers beat no path, and the option lapsed.

But 1927 was a different story. Rodgers and Hart had written scores for eight shows, seven of them hits. Lew Fields and Lyle D. Andrews, still cherishing fond memories of *Peggy Ann*, lost no time in producing this latest Fields-Hart-Rodgers opus. After an introductory tryout in the appropriately located city of Stamford, Connecticut, and a brief visit to Philadelphia, *A Connecticut Yankee* opened at the Vanderbilt Theatre on November 3, 1927. William

Gaxton was the Yank; Constance Carpenter—currently playing Anna in *The King and I*—played Alisande le Carteloise (Alice Carter in the prologue); Nana Bryant was Queen Morgan le Fay (Fay Morgan in the prologue); and William Norris played Merlin.

The combination of Fields's skillful adaptation of the Mark Twain story, plus some of Rodgers and Hart's best songs, and a superb cast, was irresistible. Atkinson of the *Times* remarked of it, "Set to as fresh and lilting songs as we may hope to find, with well-turned lyrics and an intelligent book . . . makes for novel amusement in the best of taste." According to Osborn of the *Evening World*, "Those three precocious children, the young Fields, Rodgers, and Hart . . . arrived last night . . . at the stage of the grand smash." ("Precocious children" indeed! Hart was thirty-two, Fields thirty, and Rodgers twenty-five.) The other critics were equally affable. All in all, *A Connecticut Yankee* was the most successful of their shows up to then. Its New York run—266 performances—did not establish an attendance record (*Dearest Enemy* outran it by twenty), but its road company was out for a year and four months. It was successfully revived in St. Louis in 1936, and in New York in 1943. Its score produced four all-time hits: "On a Desert Isle with Thee," "Thou Swell" (snubbed at the tryout), "I Feel at Home with You," and, of course, "My Heart Stood Still," which Rodgers and Hart, knowing a hit when they heard one, had bought back from Cochran's *One Dam Thing* for a thousand pounds.

*She's My Baby*, which ushered in the year 1928 (January 3, at the Globe), had everything—on paper. The

authors of the book were the same Bolton-Kalmar-Ruby
team that had been so successful with *Lido Lady*; that the
lyrics and music would be equally so was a foregone conclusion. The producer, Charles Dillingham, was reckoned
one of the smartest in town. The dazzling cast, headed by
the one and only Beatrice Lillie, included Irene Dunne
and Clifton Webb.

But the public said no, echoing the verdict of the critics
who, apparently bent on proving that they were not biased
in favor of Rodgers and Hart, gleefully went to work with
hobnailed boots—"a wonderwork of inaninity" . . .
"a ludicrous trifle" . . . "wretched enough" . . . "a farce so
stale that it is musty." The unfortunate baby succumbed
after nine weeks.

But Rodgers and Hart had not yet finished with 1928.
On April 26, less than two months after *Baby* had passed
on, Lew Fields produced *Present Arms* at his newly acquired Mansfield Theatre. This time it was the ever re-
liable Herbert Fields who had written the book. The setting
was one that Rodgers was to encounter some time later—
the South Pacific—and the hero was a Marine stationed
at Pearl Harbor. But no war came into the story. Nobody
was thinking about war. Mussolini had taken over Italy
six years before, but nobody took him very seriously. Hitler
was unknown outside of Germany, and the Japanese were
considered a polite and ingenious little people. True, the
villain of the piece was a German, but the worst he raised
were pineapples.

As if to make up for the drubbing they had administered
to *She's My Baby*, the critics leaned over *forward* to give

the new show good notices. Alison Smith's review in the New York *World* was typically favorable and rather shrewd: ". . . Underneath the familiar structure is the intermittent glimmer of mockery which emerges with every plot touched by this irreverent trio . . . a quality further enhanced by the persuasive melodies of Rodgers!" While *Present Arms* broke no records, it did have an excellent run—five months—and left behind at least one more Rodgers and Hart all-timer, "You Took Advantage of Me."

But 1928 had not yet finished with Fields and Rodgers and Hart. They conceived the idea—later found to be erroneous—that Charles Petit's novel, *The Son of the Grand Eunuch*, would make a good musical comedy. At least, two of them did. Rodgers still maintains that he loathed the idea, but was outnumbered. In any case, three days after the closing of *Present Arms*—September 25, to be exact—*Chee-Chee*, book by Herbert Fields, music and lyrics by Rodgers and Hart, made its bow at Lew Fields's Mansfield Theatre. The plot concerned the efforts of the devoted wife of Li-Pi-Tchou, son of the Grand Eunuch, to prevent his succeeding his father in fact as well as in name. There is no point in quoting the critics at length. "I commend it to those who love unprintable situations" . . . "dull, and in most respects nasty" will do as typical reactions. *Chee-Chee* did establish one record. It had the shortest run—three weeks and four days—of any Rodgers and Hart production before or afterward.

The dismayed silence that followed the closing of *Chee-Chee* was finally broken, after four and a half months, by *Spring Is Here,* which opened at the Alvin Theatre on

45

March 11, 1929. The Fieldses *père et fils,* were still, presumably, stanching their wounds, for the new piece had a new author, Owen Davis, and two new producers, Alex Aarons and Vinton Freedley. It was a gay tale of unrequited love that got itself requited, and it pleased everybody— including the critics, who seemed glad of the chance to kiss and make up. The *Times* proclaimed it "an impudent and endlessly amusing musical comedy," to which the *American* added that it was "a romp that is funny and lively and exultantly full of youth." The *Herald Tribune,* in a minority report, called it "a routine musical comedy of the usual type," which was offset by the *Post*'s announcement that "either Mr. Davis' book . . . or the Hart and Rodgers lyrics and music alone would have made a very pleasant evening." The *Post*'s verdict was prophetic; for at least two numbers from the score, "Yours Sincerely" and "With a Song in My Heart," have been contributing to pleasant evenings for twenty-four years.

Incidentally, *Spring Is Here* was the first Rodgers and Hart show to be made into a picture. Warner Brothers presented it at the Strand in the spring of 1930.

Aarons and Freedley must have felt that the number eleven was a lucky date for an opening; for on November 11 (short for Armistice Day) they presented *Heads Up,* another Rodgers and Hart offering, with a book by John McGowan and Paul Gerard Smith. Thirteen days before, the stock market had crashed; but *Heads Up* didn't. With Ray Bolger and Victor Moore heading the proceedings it fared well; and when it finally closed, the following February, it bequeathed two more specimens to the Rodgers and

Hart permanent collection, "Why Do You Suppose" and "A Ship Without a Sail."

Meanwhile, Florenz Ziegfeld had been considering the advisability of producing a vehicle that would exploit the personality and entertainment potentialities of—let's put it more simply: Ziegfeld decided to build a show around Ed Wynn. (It wasn't exactly a daredevil decision, assuming that Mr. Ziegfeld had seen Wynn in *The Perfect Fool*.) *Simple Simon* was its name, and it opened on February 18, 1930. The authorship of the book was shared by Mr. Wynn and Guy Bolton; lyrics and music by the indefatigable two. The great Joseph Urban designed the scenery. Besides Ed Wynn, the cast of forty-six included Bobbie Arnst, Lennox Pawle, Harriet Hoctor, and Ruth Etting. The last-named, who had jumped into the role of Sal one day before the New York opening, stopped the show with "Ten Cents a Dance." The notices were mixed, ranging from Arthur (*Herald Tribune*) Ruhl's "a large, radiant, and altogether attractive show," to John Mason (*Post*) Brown's rather crossly put "negligible in its music and lyrics . . . sadly in want of a book."

It is doubtful whether Richard Rodgers even saw the notices. His thoughts must have been elsewhere than upon *Simple Simon*. Just where will necessitate interrupting the progress of this narrative to go back several years.

In the days of Dick's extreme youth the William Rodgers family and the Ben Feiner family were old friends, and Dick and Ben, Jr., were playmates. When Ben was five years old he contracted typhoid fever, and Dr. Rodgers attended him. One afternoon when Ben was safely convalescing, Dick paid him a visit—which, as it turned out, was destined to be a momentous one, on two counts. Count one, Ben's head had been shaved, and Dick spent most of the afternoon in awe-struck contemplation of his comrade's denuded poll. Count two, at some time during the visit, Ben's new baby sister, Dorothy, was wheeled out to be duly exclaimed over and admired. The two boys, alone, maintained an Olympian aloofness—which was understandable enough. After all, a youth of five summers and a young gentleman of seven could scarcely be expected to moon over a two-month-old infant.

During the years that followed, the infant's path and Dick's frequently crossed, without provoking any particular excitement. The discrepancy in years between a fourteen-year-old boy and a seven-year-old girl is—in the boy's opinion, at least—approximately that existing between an octogenarian and a five-year-old child. However, as time passed, the gap between the two gradually narrowed until, when she was seventeen and he was twenty-four, "the trouble started," according to him, "when Larry and I had finished *Lido Lady* in London, and were coming home on the *Majestic* in September of 1926. The Feiner family were also aboard, and Dorothy and I got to sitting up nights on the boat deck."

Arriving home, young Miss Feiner matriculated at Wellesley College, where her academic duties necessarily rendered her visits to New York less frequent than young Mister Rodgers would have wished. Something must be done—and was. After a year and a half he managed to talk her into leaving college and coming back to New York.

At the end of another year and a half, when he was twenty-seven, he finally forgave her for being seven years younger. On March 5, 1930, just fifteen days after the opening of *Simple Simon*, Dorothy Feiner and Richard Rodgers were married. They still are.

Their honeymoon was spent in London, where they rented a house in Regent's Park. Lorenz Hart shared the house, and the two went to work on the lyrics and music of *Evergreen*, a new musical for C. B. Cochran. Benn Levy, best known here, perhaps, as the author of *Clutterbuck* and *Springtime for Henry*, wrote the book—the tale of a hitherto unsuccessful singer who achieves fame and fortune by masquerading as her own rejuvenated grandmother (the career of the late Fanny Ward, in reverse, may have suggested the idea). That chore accomplished, the Hart-Rodgers entourage set sail for America and Hollywood, to make their first venture into pictures. There they had the satisfaction of working again with Herbert Fields, who supplied the original screen story. It was a Warner Brothers production, entitled *The Hot Heiress*, which drew pleasant notices when it was released, about a year later. The "score" for the picture must have presented no difficulties to Rodgers and Hart, since it consisted of exactly three songs which need not detain us.

With the *Heiress* out of the way, the two commuted back to London to attend rehearsals of *Evergreen*. Dorothy Rodgers did not accompany them, being absorbed in preparations for the terrestrial debut of Mary Rodgers.

*Evergreen* opened at the Adelphi in London on December 3, 1930, with a cast headed by Jessie Matthews,

49

Sonnie Hale, and Joyce Barbour. The hit of the show was Miss Matthews' rendition of "Dancing on the Ceiling," in a set whose main feature was a huge chandelier pointing upward. The show had a great success, and ran for eight months. Five years later it was equally successful as a Gaumont British picture, but for some reason has never been produced here in the round, so to speak. "Dancing on the Ceiling" became popular despite the activities of radio's guardians of public morals, who banned it for a while because the word "bed" occurs twice in the verse and once in the refrain.

Meanwhile the lyrico-musical team had returned to America to carry out a contract they had with Schwab and Mandel for a new production. The fruit of their labors, *America's Sweetheart*, opened at the Broadhurst Theatre on February 10, 1931. The book, by Herbert Fields (the last he was to write with them), was, as you might guess from the title, a satire on Hollywood. Harriet Lake (Ann Sothern to you) played the heroine, with Jack Whiting as the hero. The songs—"happily phrased, insinuatingly clever and rememberable" (Gabriel, New York *American*) —attracted most of the attention. "There is a rush about the music and a mocking touch in the lyrics that make the score more deftly satirical than the production" (Atkinson, the *Times*). At least one number, "I've Got Five Dollars," is still with us.

Then Hollywood beckoned. Paramount suggested that they come out West to write music for pictures, offering princely inducements. The offer sounded tempting, particularly since it offered a chance to experiment with a new medium. Sound pictures were only four years old; their possibilities were still largely unexplored. Besides, memories of *The Hot Heiress* were happy ones, and offered prospects of congenial work in pleasant surroundings. Accordingly, in the spring of 1931, Hart and the Rodgers family moved to the Coast.

Their first assignment went well. The picture was *Love Me Tonight*, a vehicle for Maurice Chevalier and Jeanette MacDonald, with a glittering supporting cast that included Charlie Ruggles, Charles Butterworth, Myrna Loy, C. Aubrey Smith, and Joseph Cawthorn. For this they wrote five songs: "Mimi," "He's Nothing but a Tailor," "Isn't It Romantic?" "Love Me Tonight," and "Lover," the last-named still being one of the most popular in the entire Rodgers and Hart repertoire.

Since there is no accurate record of the dates on which Rodgers and Hart finished work on the various pictures they scored, let the films be listed here by the dates on which they were released in New York. *Love Me Tonight* made its bow at the Rivoli Theatre on August 18, 1932. Their next, released in September of that year, was another Paramount production, *The Phantom President*, starring George M. Cohan, with Claudette Colbert and Jimmy Durante also among those present. The three songs they wrote attracted no attention.

Next came *Hallelujah, I'm a Bum!* starring Al Jolson, written some time in '32 and released by United Artists at the Rivoli on February 8, 1933. Here the pair had a chance to do the experimenting that they had been waiting for. In addition to writing five songs for the picture ("You Are

Too Beautiful," still a favorite, was one of them), they evolved what they called "rhythmic dialogue," whereby most of the dialogue was written in rhyme and sung. They had tried it tentatively in a scene or two in *Love Me Tonight,* and now they went all out. The experiment had its moments, but tended to slow down the action.

*Manhattan Melodrama,* produced by David Selznik and released at the Capitol in May of 1934, had an all-star cast that included Clark Gable, Bill Powell, Myrna Loy, and Mickey Rooney. The Rodgers and Hart contribution was a solitary song, "The Bad in Every Man." Under the title of "Oh, Lord, Make Me a Motion Picture Star" it had been dropped from a Jean Harlow picture, and was in turn discarded from *Manhattan Melodrama.* Undismayed, the pair later took it to Jack Robbins, the music publisher. "It's a nice tune, boys," quoth the words-and-music man, "but it needs a more romantic lyric, and a better title." In due course they brought it back and saw it published. Under the title of "Blue Moon" it sold 175,000 copies and has remained one of their best sellers.

In *Words and Music,* the Rodgers-and-Hart film biography that was produced in 1948, five years after Hart's death, he is represented as living in a Beverly Hills mansion so huge that its living room had an echo. This is a pardonable exaggeration. It wasn't the house that was so large. Hart, a passionate swimmer, had simply rented the house that had the largest swimming pool that he could find. Here, every Sunday, a group of aquatic *aficionados* would gather for luncheon. On occasion the group would number a hundred guests, including the Olympic swimming team, whose stellar attraction was a lovely girl named Eleanor Holm.

The Rodgers mansion was slightly less stately, but it —or, rather, they, for the family rented more than one —decidedly sufficed. Altogether, life in Hollywood was a luxurious one, and a tranquil one.

"Hollywood" is a grossly misused word, a generic term covering Hollywood, Beverly Hills, Bel Air, Brentwood, Westwood, Pacific Palisades, and Santa Monica. It is inhabited by the natives, who follow all sorts of callings, and the movie people, who constitute a world apart and live in houses that they rent from people who rented them from the people who built them. If you are connected with the making of pictures you rise at six or seven, are "on the set" at nine, and work until six, with an hour out for lunch, where you discuss pictures with your fellow workers. In the evening you go to a dinner party, at which you have been implored not to be later than eight. You arrive at eight, and the hostess is in the bathtub. At dinner you discuss pictures with your fellow workers, plus some speculation as to whether whose option is going to be taken up. By ten-thirty all the working guests go home, since they must get up early. The following evening you repeat the performance, with a different hostess. And so on.

In other words, the tranquil life of Hollywood can be lethally boresome if you're not busy. There are no long walks in the country. There isn't any country. You seldom see a tree that wasn't planted, and except for a few weeks in winter you never see running water. The populous areas are vomiting vegetation (irrigated), the unpopulous,

53

sand and sage brush. There are no footpaths along the boulevards. So help me, pedestrians at night have been known to be stopped by the suspicious Beverly Hills police, demanding to know why they were afoot. You cannot even attend a movie matinee, because the movie houses in this movie capital of the world don't open until 6:00 P.M. You can swim or play tennis just so long. Two things make life tolerable over any extended stretch of time: people— God help you if you know no people—and work, hard, congenial work. All of which goes to explain why, despite the lovely pay checks and the life of ease, the team of Rodgers and Hart began to exhibit symptoms of being fed up.

They had come to Hollywood in 1931. It was now the spring of 1934. They had been in Hollywood nearly three years, during which they had been allowed to write just sixteen songs. Judging from their pre-Hollywood average of three shows a year, they could have supplied lyrics and music for six Broadway productions in that length of time. They were living in Luxury's justly celebrated lap, but they weren't doing anything.

The end came when Rodgers read a seven-word item in O. O. McIntyre's column in the Los Angeles *Examiner*: "What ever became of Rodgers and Hart?" That tore it. They worked out their contract with M-G-M, and then, as Rodgers puts it, "We climbed aboard The Chief and came back to the United States."

It took courage to make the move. For two years and ten months, ever since the closing night of *America's Sweetheart*, nothing by Rodgers and Hart had been heard in a "legitimate" theater. They had been rated the top song-writing team on Broadway; but Broadway has a cruelly short memory. Other writers of words and music had passed through Hollywood's iron curtain and been forgotten. That might be their fate.

There was another problem, an economic one. When you live in a community where your next-door neighbors on either side have annual incomes running into six figures, it is virtually impossible *not* to return their hospitality, *not* to maintain their scale of living. No matter how much you make, by the time Hollywood and the director of internal revenue are through with you, your savings are not impressive. When they arrived in New York, the Rodgers family were faced with these alternatives: either to lower their standard of living while waiting for a break—and incidentally, the advent of Linda Rodgers at that moment was not an inexpensive occasion—or borrow. Rodgers chose the second, the only possible one.

On Broadway, as in Hollywood, the unforgivable sin is to seem to be in need of a job. Once you show symptoms of looking for work, the pack does not do the kindly thing, turn on you and tear you to pieces. It does something worse; it crosses the street when it sees you coming. Rodgers could not take a job without destroying the prestige he had built up over nine years. Selling babies' underwear was definitely out. He could not hang around the producers' offices, as he and Hart had done in their early days. The producers had been coming to him too long for that. And he could not economize. All he could do was wait. The wait lasted a year and seven months, at the end of which he was $34,000 in debt.[2]

When the break did come, it was a spectacular one.

For years the New York Hippodrome occupied the same position in New York's amusement world that the Radio City Music Hall commands today: It was a place to take the children, on the pretense that you only went for their sakes; and it was a "must" for out-of-town visitors. For most of its existence it provided no movies, of course; but it provided just about everything else in the way of spectacular entertainment, including a herd of elephants. Its huge stage contained an equally huge tank, into whose waters a squad of dancers and chorines marched, twice a day, never to emerge. In later years its fortunes declined (the heavy competition of the Music Hall was one cause), and it was finally torn down. A budding skyscraper now occupies the spot upon which it once stood.

It was, however, still standing in 1935, when it attracted the speculative eye of Billy Rose. Mr. Rose, a small man with large ideas, having been in the night-club business for some time, had recently opened Billy Rose's Café de Paris, the first theater-restaurant in New York, and was casting about for some new outlet for his abundant energies. The Hippodrome filled the bill admirably. It was big, and it was available. All it needed was something to put into it.

Accordingly, if you had been walking down Sixth Avenue in the fall of '35 on your way to Forty-second Street, you could hardly have escaped seeing enormous signs plastered on the marque of the Hippodrome, admonishing the

[2] Don't worry. He has since paid it back.

passer-by: "SH-SH-SH! JUMBO IS REHEARSING." What on earth was *Jumbo*?

We found out on the evening of November 16, 1935, when the Hippodrome revealed what Percy Hammond of the *Herald Tribune* called "a sane and exciting compound of opera, animal show, folk drama, harlequinade, carnival, circus, extravaganza, and spectacle." *Jumbo* was all of that, and more. It exploited the talents of bareback riders, clowns, a juggler, a contortionist, wire-walkers, trapeze performers, ax-throwers, Camilla's Birds, and Stanley's Bears. Also present were Paul Whiteman and his orchestra, playing on a tall platform upstage, and Big Rosie, a mild and gigantic lady elephant. Heading the cast was Jimmy Durante.

There was even a plot, a Romeo-Juliet story of the amours of the respective daughter and son of two rival circus proprietors, concocted by the impish team of Hecht and MacArthur. Most important of all, in the minds of many, *Jumbo* marked the return of Rodgers and Hart. Asked why he had thought of them, after so long an absence from the stage, Mr. Rose remarks, simply, "They were tops in their field, so I got 'em. I wouldn't have cared if they hadn't had a show in ten years." His belief was amply justified. *Jumbo* ran its course—nine months at the Hippodrome and two months at the Texas Centennial in Forth Worth— and is now one with Nineveh and Tyre. But three of its numbers, "My Romance," "The Most Beautiful Girl in the World," and "Little Girl Blue," are as contemporary as they were the day they were written.

The success of *Jumbo* was a triumphant answer to O. O. McIntyre's question of a year and a half before. Rodgers and Hart were again doing business at the old stand. Their next offering was *On Your Toes*, a satire on the ballet. The book, by Rodgers and Hart and revised by George Abbott, had been rejected by a Hollywood studio as a vehicle for Fred Astaire. The Shuberts took an option on it, but let it lapse. It was promptly picked up by Dwight Deere Wiman, who produced it at the Imperial Theatre on April 13, 1936, while *Jumbo* was still running. Worthington Miner (lately director of television's "Studio One") staged the book, with George Balanchine directing the ballet numbers. Ray Bolger ("a jazz Nijinsky," as Robert Garland called him) and Tamara Geva shared the leads, with a supporting cast that included Luella Gear and Monty Woolley—beard and all.

There are several "firsts" connected with *On Your Toes*. As noted above, it was the first musical comedy of which Rodgers and Hart had a hand in fashioning the book as well as the lyrics and music. The part of Phil Dolan III was Ray Bolger's first leading role. Also, it was the first show of its kind in which a ballet was an essential part of the plot. It was the first Rodgers and Hart production to top the three hundred mark in performances (315—nine months—to be exact), and the first of theirs to be exported to London. Of the score, still to be heard are "It's Got to Be Love," "There's a Small Hotel," and, of course, the famous "Slaughter on Tenth Avenue" ballet.

After a flying visit to the West Coast, where they wrote two numbers, "When You're Dancing the Waltz" and "Are You My Love?" for a technicolor picture called *Dancing Pirate*, the two returned to New York, where they went to work on the first all-Rodgers and Hart production, *Babes in Arms*.

This was a play within a play. The story: that of a group of youngsters, the children of old-time troupers, who, in order to escape being relegated to a children's home, stage a revue of their own. Dwight Deere Wiman, the producer, brought it to the Shubert Theatre almost one year to the day—April 14, 1937—after the launching of *On Your Toes*.

*Babes in Arms* was a story about kids, and it had a cast of kids, most of them unknown. Among them, they handled eleven numbers, five of them among the best songs that Rodgers and Hart ever wrote. Seventeen-year-old Mitzi Green sang "Where or When" and "The Lady Is a Tramp." Wynn Murray, equally youthful, sang "My Funny Valentine" and "Johnny One Note," while Grace McDonald and Rolly Pickert took charge of "I Wish I Were [note Hart's meticulous use of the subjunctive] in Love Again." Twenty-three-year-old Alfred (*Oklahoma!*) Drake and Robert Rounseville, now a star tenor of the New York City Opera Company, sang in two concerted numbers, but made no solo appearances.

All in all, their first venture as sole authors was a happy one. The critics called it "a fresh, youthful, and utterly captivating show" . . . "a zestful, tuneful, and brilliantly danced affair" . . . "a book that is full of good feeling, and a score that is altogether superb." It ran for nine months, closing on December 18, 1937.

It was still running, as a matter of fact, when their next offering, *I'd Rather Be Right*, appeared. Sam H. Harris brought it into the Alvin Theatre on November 2. The book was the work of another team, George S. Kaufman and Moss Hart, whose *You Can't Take It with You* had been a sensational success of the previous season. Its story concerned a young couple who were anxious to be married, but could only do so if the boy got a raise in salary, which could happen only if the President succeeded in balancing the budget. Hampered by the Postmaster General (Paul Parks), the Secretary of the Treasury (Taylor Holmes), the Chief Justice (John Cherry), the Chief Justice's girl (Mary Jane Walsh), and others, the President (George M. Cohan) never did get around to balancing the budget; but he advised the youngsters to marry anyhow—which they did. The satire on the New Deal administration was about as subtle as a blow with a blunt instrument, but it delighted the customers to the tune of an eleven-months' run. Brooks Atkinson, of the *Times,* pronounced it "playful . . . hardly enough for a first-class musical show"; whereas Burns Mantle, of the *News,* drawing a deep breath, called it "one of the most important plays of this generation." The rest were somewhere between the two extremes. John Mason Brown, of the *Post,* wrote that "Richard Rodgers' music seems to be more serviceable than catchy," a remark that, despite its disparaging tone, has interesting implications.

The average musical comedy of the twenties and thirties possessed a plot whose chief function was to provide something upon which to hang songs—much as strings of popcorn are festooned upon a Christmas tree.[3] The songs were

[3] As the gnat might have said to Alice, "You might make a joke on that—something about 'pop' songs and 'corn,' you know."

offered for their own sakes, written with one eye upon sheet music sales and the other on recordings. When it came to providing the score, the composer dug some leftovers out of the barrel, then met his quota with such tunes as would guarantee so many fast numbers, so many slow ones, so many waltzes—and so on. The chief aim of the lyrist[4] was to provide words that could be sung anywhere, regardless of the plot. The result was something that was less a score than an anthology. A given song could be taken out of the first act and transposed to the second, with no one the wiser. It could be sung out of context because there was *no* context.

Almost from the beginning, Rodgers and Hart had worked on the assumption that the story is as important as the score. The stories they picked had some substance of their own, something more than the usual boy-meets-girl formula. Shows like *Dearest Enemy, Peggy Ann, A Connecticut Yankee, Present Arms, On Your Toes, Babes in Arms*—these were not just run-of-the-mill plots. Moreover, most of the Rodgers and Hart scores contain numbers that are directly connected with the story, songs that cannot be sung out of context. Consider some of the song titles from *I'd Rather Be Right*: "A Homogeneous Cabinet," "A Little Bit of Constitutional Fun," "We're Going to Balance the Budget," "Labor Is the Thing," "Off the Record," "A Baby Bond." Not many of these could have been intended for the night-club trade. Only one song out of the entire score, "Have You Met Miss Jones?" could be called a hit.

[4] I said "lyrist." "Lyricist" is a Broadway corruption not to be found in any dictionary.

Yet Brown was righter than he knew when he called Rodgers' music "serviceable." It helped to prolong the run of the piece, even if it didn't sell an avalanche of printed copies.

Another characteristic of their work together underlines their fundamental respect for the theater. The musical comedy score of those days comprised eighteen numbers, including reprises. There might, on occasion, be seventeen, or nineteen, or even twenty. But the traditional number was eighteen.

Consider Rodgers and Hart. Not counting *The Poor Little Ritz Girl*, which was not entirely their own, they wrote words and music for twenty-seven musical comedies, with an average of *thirteen* numbers for each show, including reprises. Their longest score, twenty-four numbers, was written for one of their direst failures, *Betsy*; their shortest, six, for another flop, *Chee-Chee*. But the average of thirteen still holds. This allowed fifteen more minutes of dialogue, and was, I am positive, at least partly responsible for their success, since it allowed the book to unfold with some degree of plausibility, to be a play, rather than a succession of song cues.

With *I'd Rather Be Right* successfully launched, the pair now entrained to Hollywood, where they had been engaged to write music for a Warner Brothers picture, *Fools for Scandal*. They worked for three months, turning out, not merely songs, but a complete musical score. The picture was released in March, 1938, with no music at all.

Meanwhile, possibly during the Hollywood stay, or at any rate early in 1938, Rodgers had read a play by a Hungarian dramatist, John Vaszary, wherein a certain Count

Palaffi, having been betrayed by a faithless fiancée, swears that he will never be married—except to an angel. The said angel promptly appears, and the Count promptly marries her, and she eventually, though not so promptly, becomes a charming mortal and a reasonably faithful wife. This sounded crazy enough to make a good movie musical, and the two promptly set to work to make a picture of it.[5]

The task was accomplished, to the accompaniment of what Rodgers terms "a good deal of incidental screaming." Both partners were convinced of the essential soundness of their respective opinions, and the process of reconciling those opinions was sometimes an arduous and bitter one. It was, however, purely professional bitterness. Outside business hours they were the close friends they always had been. Rodgers has some interesting comments, however, regarding the creation of Hart's lyrics.

A vast quantity of ink and conversation has been spilled regarding Larry Hart's fanatical aesthetic integrity, his tireless search for the right word, the odd rhyme. In his own account of how he wrote a lyric, as quoted in *The Rodgers and Hart Song Book*, he said:

If I am trying to write a melodic song hit, I let Richard Rodgers get his tune first. Then I take the most distinctive melodic phrase in his tune, and work on that. Next I try to find the meaning of that phrase and to develop a euphonic set of words to fit it.

According to Rodgers, this rather high-flown obiter dictum is something less than accurate. It was not a question of *letting* him write the tune first. He wrote the tune

---

[5] It was made for M-G-M, which promptly shelved it. They had to dicker to get the stage rights.

first for virtually all their songs. Hart hated work—who doesn't?—and it took the challenge of an existing tune to rouse him to his best efforts.

Confronted with the task of writing a lyric "cold"—that is, with no melody on which to hang it—he was, in Rodgers' words, "a maddeningly careless craftsman, who would settle for anything." Moreover, once he had finished a lyric, wild horses—to say nothing of a wild composer—could not have induced him to change it. If there was an obscene rhyme to a given word, Hart would use it. Any objection would be met with "What's wrong with it? It rhymes, doesn't it?"

If the anguished Rodgers pointed out that you can't say such things in the theater, he would be dismissed with an airy "Why not? Just because nobody has ever done it?"

So, wearily, Rodgers would provide a tune, and the two would work out the lyric together.

It may have been an exasperating system, but it produced results. One of the more endearing results was unveiled on the evening of May 11, 1938, when Dwight Deere Wiman produced *I Married an Angel* at the Shubert Theatre in New York. The stage director was Joshua Logan —a name to be closely allied with Rodgers' more recent career. Dennis King was a dashing Count Palaffi, the role of the Angel was enchantingly played and danced by a young Norwegian girl born Eva Brigitta Hartwig but possibly better known as Vera Zorina; and Vivienne Segal and Walter Slezak made their first appearances in a Rodgers and Hart show. The score was one of Rodgers' best, and

*64*

contained at least two memorable hits: "I Married an Angel" and "Spring Is Here."

The critics scraped the barrel for adjectives: "bright . . . bubbling . . . imaginative . . . opulent . . . tuneful . . . charming . . . satisfying . . . intoxicating . . . extraordinarily beautiful." Brooks Atkinson, of the *Times*, obviously fresh from seeing *The Green Pastures*, remarked, "Musical comedy has met its masters, and they have reared back and passed a Forty-fourth Street miracle." Everybody was happy, and the show had a longer run—338 performances —than any previous Rodgers and Hart offering. Be it noted, incidentally, that it was an equal success when it played the Theatre Royal in Sydney, Australia, in a version in which Melton Moore, playing the Dennis King role, not only sang his allotted numbers, but also obliged with excerpts from Romberg's *Maytime* and Friml's *The Vagabond King*!

With a smash hit running briskly at the Shubert, there seemed to be little risk of the public's forgetting Rodgers and Hart. Nevertheless, the team were taking no chances. On November 23, with the *Angel* still three months to go, *The Boys from Syracuse* put in an appearance at the Alvin. The book of this one was the fruit of an interesting collaboration by William Shakespeare and George Abbott. Mr. Abbott also produced and directed the show, which was a highly irreverent adaptation of *A Comedy of Errors*. Mr. Shakespeare took no active part in the proceedings—although there is an unfounded rumor that on the night of the New York opening a low, moaning cry was heard ema-

nating from the chancel of the parish church in Stratford-
on-Avon.

Regardless of Mr. Shakespeare's feelings in the matter,
he had a hit on his hands. The piece was beautifully cast,
with Ronald Graham and Eddie Albert as the two Antiph-
oluses (Antipholi, perhaps?), and Teddy Hart and
Jimmy Savo as the two Dromios. Muriel Angelus was
Ronald Graham's wife, Adrianna, Marcy Westcott was her
sister, Luciana, and Burl Ives came out from behind his
guitar to be a tailor's apprentice. The score was "grade-A
Rodgers and Hart," and included such all-time hits as "This
Can't Be Love," "Sing for Your Supper," and one of the
loveliest waltz songs ever written by anybody, "Falling in
Love with Love."

The critics had to send out for fresh adjectives. As
Brooks Atkinson announced, "Mr. Abbott has a knack of
giving everything he touches freshness, spontaneity, and
spinning pace. Rodgers and Hart have written him a ver-
satile score . . . some of their gayest songs . . . a beautiful
feast of rollicking mummery." Sidney Whipple, of the
*World-Telegram*, remarked, simply, "I believe it will be
regarded as the greatest musical comedy of its time," and
let it go at that.

If this chronicle were a play instead of a biography, it
would be instantly criticized as having no conflict. In the
fourteen years that Rodgers and Hart had been working on
Broadway they had had twenty hits and just three misses.
A tale of such almost uninterrupted success is bound to
possess a certain degree of monotony. The Greeks grew so
tired of hearing Aristides referred to as "The Just" that they

finally threw him out of Athens; and the twosome's colleagues, who were, after all, only human, must have had a
sneaking hope that the law of averages would catch up with
them. Momentarily, it looked as if the colleagues were going
to get their wish; for the next Rodgers and Hart show, *Too
Many Girls*, had a disastrous dress rehearsal in New Haven.

But no. When the show opened at the Imperial Theatre,
on October 18, 1939, its wrinkles had all been ironed out
—and it was just another hit. Two Georges were involved
in the production: George Marion, Jr., who wrote the
book, and George Abbott, who produced and directed the
piece. The plot concerned a millionaire who sends his
daughter, Consuelo, to Pottawatomie College at Stop Gap,
New Mexico, and hires four all-American football heroes
to act as her bodyguard, without telling her so. Compli-
cations. Satisfactory ending. The cast included Desi Arnaz,
Richard Kollmar, Diosa Costello, and one Van Johnson,
who played an anonymous student. At least two numbers
from the score, "I Didn't Know What Time It Was"
and "Give It Back to the Indians," were destined to belong
to the ages. The only break in the unanimity of the critics
was supplied by the *Post,* which hailed the score as containing "some of the most enchanting music the gifted Mr.
Rodgers has written," and *Time* magazine, which announced that "good as it is, the music is not Rodgers at
quite his best or most individual."

On November 12, following the opening of *Too Many
Girls,* a new ballet by Rodgers, *Ghost Town,* was produced at the Metropolitan Opera House by the Ballet Russe
de Monte Carlo, the composer conducting. The scenario,

by Rodgers and Marc Platoff, depicted the extravagant rise and spectacular fall of a mining town in the Sierras. It had seven performances in New York, was played all during a country-wide tour, and had another performance at the Metropolitan the following spring.

At last the law of averages did catch up—although the blow was more a love tap than a knockout. The party of the first part was *Higher and Higher*, which Dwight Deere Wiman brought to the Shubert Theatre on April 4, 1940. It had Pygmalion-type book (the maidservant of a bankrupt gentleman being trained to marry a rich playboy) by Gladys Hurlbut and Joshua Logan, "based on an idea by Irvin Pincus" (Shaw got no billing). Mr. Logan also directed. Jack Haley played the lead, with Marta Eggerth playing a part that had been intended for Zorina. Robert Rounseville, the operatic tenor, doubled in the small parts of the soda jerker and a truckman, but was not allowed to sing. The score contained at least one outstanding ditty, "It Never Entered My Mind," whose verse is a remote ancestor of "The Surrey with the Fringe on Top." The critics were amiable, though not delirious.

The real star of the show turned out to be a seal. Miss Hurlbut discovered him at the animal fair held in Woodstock, New York, for the benefit of the local library, and persuaded Mr. Logan that he would be a valuable member of the cast. His name was Sharkey, and he was a graduate of Huling's Seal College at Kingston-on-the-Hudson, from which come most of the better-trained seals. His specialty was what might be termed backbiting. But even with Mr. Haley's admirable support, Sharkey's routine turned out

Here is the cast of *Babes in Arms,* which included Mitzi Green, Ray Heatherton, Alfred Drake. Mitzi Green sang "The Lady Is a Tramp" and together with Ray Heatherton "Where or When," both lasting favorites. *Babes in Arms* had a successful run of 289 performances, after opening at the Shubert Theatre in April, 1937.

*On Your Toes* ran from April, 1936, to January, 1937. Here Ray Bolger, Tamara Geva and George Church dance the well-known ballet "Slaughter on Tenth Avenue." Ray Bolger's dancing in the role of Phil Dolan III caused one critic to describe him as a jazz Nijinsky. ( Culver Service.)

*I Married an Angel*, staged by Joshua Logan, opened in May of 1938, only closed after 338 performances. Left, Vivienne Segal and Walter Slezak make their first appearance in a Rodgers and Hart show. Right, Vera Zorina plays an angel with Dennis King as a

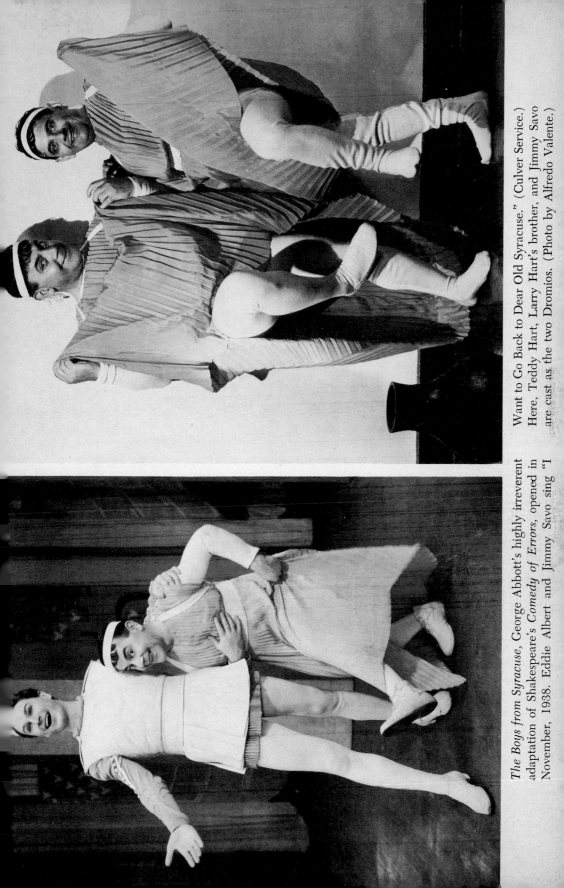

*The Boys from Syracuse*, George Abbott's highly irreverent adaptation of Shakespeare's *Comedy of Errors*, opened in November, 1938. Eddie Albert and Jimmy Savo sing "I Want to Go Back to Dear Old Syracuse." (Culver Service.) Here, Teddy Hart, Larry Hart's brother, and Jimmy Savo are cast as the two Dromios. (Photo by Alfredo Valente.)

This rehearsal picture, above, of *Too Many Girls* shows composer Rodgers as a musician. The show opened in October, 1939, and had a successful run of 249 performances. Below, Rodgers and Hart talk with Marta Eggerth, star of *Higher and Higher*. A run of 108 performances did not take this show out of the red.

*Pal Joey*, one of the best known of all Rodgers and Hart musicals, opened in May of 1941. Here is Gene Kelly, who sang and danced the lead in the original production, which had a total of 374 New York performances. The blond young man in the background is Van Johnson. (Courtesy of Rodgers and Hammerstein.) On the right is Vivienne Segal, who sang the famous "Bewitched, Bothered and Bewildered" and played the lead opposite Mr. Kelly in the first production and opposite Harold Lang in the 1952 revival. (Photo by Eileen Darby.) In *Pal Joey*, Rodgers and Hart with George Abbott, producer, broke with tradition by bringing complete realism to the musical comedy stage, with a book based on John O'Hara's series in *The New Yorker* about a cheap gigolo. Critical and popular acclaim showed them that this was what the public enjoyed.

*By Jupiter* came to the Shubert Theatre on June 2, 1942, and had the longest Rodgers and Hart run of one year and ten days. Ray Bolger is shown here as Sapiens, the meek husband of Amazon Hippolyta, played by Benay Venuta. With the writing of *By Jupiter*, the long partnership between Richard Rodgers and Lorenz Hart was ended.

Here, composer Richard Rodgers conducts his own works with the St. Louis Municipal Orchestra.

Above, Richard Rodgers with his father, Dr. William A. Rodgers, perhaps the earliest supporter of his son's career as a composer. Below, Richard Rodgers with his wife Dorothy and a favorite pet in their Connecticut house. (Photo by Phillipe Halsman.)

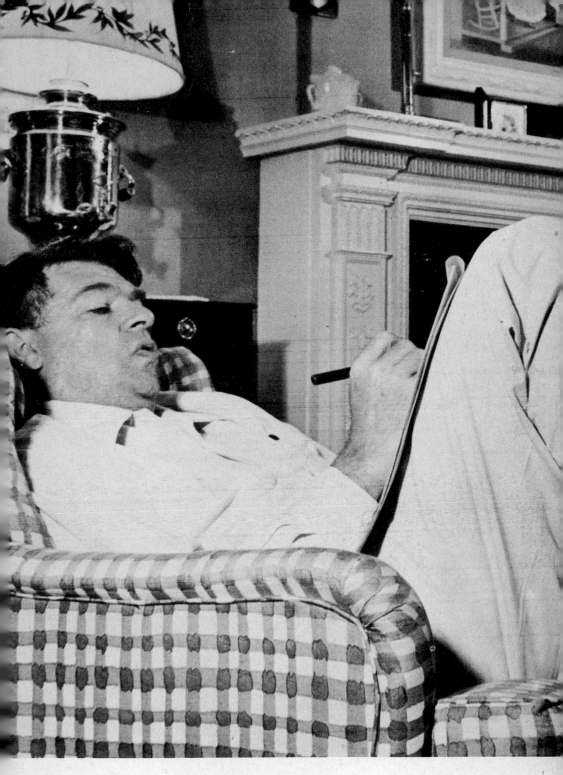

Oscar Hammerstein II

Oscar Hammerstein I, grandfather of Oscar II, well-known impresario, who made his fortune through the invention of a cigar-making machine, above left. (Alfred Davis Collection.) Right, he sits elegantly top-hatted in his office. (Culver Service.) Below, he is shown with Mary Garden, who did her famous Dance of the Seven Veils in Salome at Hammerstein's Manhattan Opera House. (Culver Service.)

Oscar I sits at a piano semicircled by composers of his day and of the present; left to right: Jerome Kern, Louis Hirsch, A. Baldwin Sloane, Rudolf Friml, Alfred Robyn, Gustave Kerker, Hugo Felix, John Philip Sousa, Leslie Stuart, Raymond Hubbell, John L. Golden, Sylvio Hein and Irving Berlin.

Theatrical interest developed in Oscar II at an early age. Here he is, above left, in a school play, and right in a Columbia University Varsity Show, which he not only played in but wrote. Below, left, Willy Hammerstein, father of Oscar II, who managed the fabulously profitable vaudeville house, Hammerstein's Victoria. Right is Arthur Hammerstein, his uncle the producer, who gave Oscar his first job in the theater. (Culver Service.)

Ed Wynn in *Sometime,* a musical comedy by Rida Johnson Young, based on a scenario by Oscar II, who also stage-managed it. The girl in the picture is Mildred Lague. (Culver Service.)

*Daffy Dill*, starring Frank Tinney and Marion Sunshine, opened in August of 1922, ran for 71 performances. Oscar II wrote all the lyrics and shared the book with Guy Bolton, music by Herbert Stothart. (Culver Service.)

to be something less than a full evening's entertainment. *Higher and Higher* closed on June 15, reopened on August 5, and closed for good on August 24. Its total New York run of 108 performances (five more than *The Girl Friend*) would have sufficed in 1926. But production costs were spiraling in 1940, and *Higher and Higher* ended on the red side of the ledger.

There is one rather odd phenomenon connected with the Rodgers and Hart output. During the first ten years of their Broadway career, that is, from *The Garrick Gaieties* up to and including *America's Sweetheart*, the two averaged, believe it or not, three shows a year; and the average run of these was five months. From *Jumbo* on, however, their pace slackened to an average of three shows every *two* years. At the same time, the shows lasted longer, having an average run of nine months. There must be a moral to to that, if one could only find it. It could be that they were taking greater pains with their lyrics and music, except that there is no evidence to support that theory. They turned out as many enduring hits during the pre-*Jumbo* period as they did in the post-*Jumbo* years. One could, however, argue with some degree of plausibility that, book-conscious from the beginning, they were becoming increasingly specific—in their own minds at least—as to the kind of book they wanted to set. And when they couldn't find what they wanted they undertook the task of providing it for themselves. It is significant, it seems to me, that their five most successful shows were all written between 1936 and 1942, and that the books of four of those five were written or adapted by Rodgers and Hart themselves. The single exception was provided by a novelist, who also had radical ideas as to what constitutes a good musical comedy.

Or perhaps it all just happened that way. In any case, nine months elapsed between the closing of *Higher and Higher* and the emergence of a new Rodgers and Hart show. It turned out to be worth waiting for.

During 1939 John O'Hara had been running a series of sketches in *The New Yorker*, in the form of letters from a singing master of ceremonies in second-rate night clubs to a bandleader friend of his. Early in 1940 he wrote to Rodgers, suggesting that the character, Pal Joey, and the orbit in which he moved might make a musical show. "I read that you two have a commitment with Dwight Wiman for a show [*Higher and Higher*] this spring, but if and when you get through with that, I do hope you like my idea."

I think it is safe to say that when *Pal Joey*, book by John O'Hara, music and lyrics by Rodgers and Hart, was produced by George Abbott at the Ethel Barrymore Theatre on May 19, 1941, it brought something quite new to the musical comedy stage: complete realism. Here was a book by a superb storyteller with an unerring ear for colloquial speech—funny, grimy, sardonic, with not a trace of whimsy or make-believe. The nearest thing to it had been *Rainbow*, written in 1928 by Laurence Stallings and Oscar Hammerstein II, which tried realism on a public that was not prepared for it. The hero of *Pal Joey* is a cheap entertainer and a gigolo, yet admittedly good at both his professions. The heroine, if you can call her such, is a Chicago matron who knows what she wants and is willing to pay for it, but can be as completely ruthless as her boy friend when she deems it advisable.

The cast was a superb one. It was headed by Gene Kelly, with everything needed to portray the little heel and congenital liar that is Joey, plus the charm that keeps him from being completely nauseating. Vivienne Segal was perfection as the libidinous Vera. June Havoc was the tough Gladys, Van Johnson was Victor, Jean Casto was Melba, the hardboiled newspaper woman, and Leila Ernst, as Linda, the only "decent" girl in the show, actually made her interesting.

Rodgers and Hart outdid themselves. Never before had they turned out a score so crammed with unforgettable words and music. O'Hara's unusual book was a challenge to which they had responded brilliantly. To list all the hit numbers would be to list the entire score. Suffice it to say that they included "I Could Write a Book," "What Is a Man?" "Happy Hunting Horn," "Bewitched, Bothered, and Bewildered," "Zip," "In Our Little Den," and "Take Him."

In view of the popular success of *Pal Joey* and the uproarious welcome it received when it was revived, eleven years and seven months later, the critics were curiously at odds concerning the original production. Richard Watts, of the *Herald Tribune*, called it "a brilliant, sardonic, and strikingly original musical comedy . . . one of Richard Rodgers' most winning scores . . . an outstanding triumph." Robert Coleman, of the *Mirror*, wrote: "It takes a lot of savvy to put over a musical whose hero is a pill, but that's just what the team of Abbott, O'Hara, Hart, and Rodgers have done . . . a hit if I ever saw one."

On the other hand, Richard Lockridge dismissed it as having "not really much plot." John Mason Brown, of the *Post*, observed that it "looked during its first half as if it were going to prove one of the season's brighter arrivals. . . . But from the moment . . . the book gained in prominence, 'Pal Joey' . . . began to slip . . . so noticeably that its slipping can only be described as a fall." Brooks Atkinson, of the *Times*, was slightly horrified: "If it is possible to make an entertaining musical comedy out of an odious story, 'Pal Joey' is it . . . a joyless book about a sulky assignation. . . . Rodgers and Hart have written the score with wit and skill . . . some scabrous lyrics by Lorenz Hart. . . . The ugly topic that is up for discussion stands between this theatre-goer and real enjoyment of a well-staged show."

Later on we shall read what some of them had to say about the revival.

*Pal Joey* closed in April, 1942, after a run of eleven months. (Incidentally, all figures in this book refer to New York runs only. There were many performances on the road, naturally, but statistics concerning them are not consistently available.) Two months later, Rodgers and Hart were ready with a new offering. It, too, had a hard-boiled central character, but there the resemblance ended. It was an adaptation by the two of Julian Thompson's play, *The Warrior's Husband*, in which Katharine Hepburn and Romney Brent had shone brilliantly eleven years before. The setting was Asia Minor in mythological days; the story,

88

that of the Amazon women at war with the men of Greece, and their final subjugation without bloodshed. Under the title of *By Jupiter* it came to the Shubert Theatre on June 2, 1942, presented by Wiman, Rodgers, and Kollmar, and staged by Joshua Logan. The cast, just right as usual, included Ray Bolger as Sapiens, the meek consort of Hippolyta (Benay Venuta), the domineering queen of the Amazons, and Antiope (Constance Moore), his ravishing sister-in-law. Ralph Dumke was Hercules, whose mission was to steal Hippolyta's girdle (not that kind of girdle), and Bob Douglas was satisfactorily mythological as Achilles. At least three of the songs—"Nobody's Heart Belongs to Me," "Ev'rything I've Got," and "Wait Till You See Her" —are still happily current.

The critics raved, the remarks of Richard Watts being typical: "A characteristically charming score, ingenious lyrics, beautiful settings and costumes, a first-rate comedian, brilliantly staged dances, and a pleasant air of festivity." It was Rodgers' first venture in the producing field, and a triumphantly successful one.

Ray Bolger's resignation from the cast, on grounds of ill health, made it necessary to close the show while it was still going strong, and made him the butt of considerable angry criticism, most of his critics claiming that he had used a pretty flimsy excuse for throwing one hundred people out of work. There were red faces on Broadway a little later, when it transpired that at the request of the USO he had made a secret flight to the South Seas to entertain the troops. And even so, *By Jupiter* had the longest run—

one year and ten days—that Rodgers and Hart had ever had. They were at the peak of their joint career.

It was the last show they were to write together. By the end of 1942 Rodgers had written *Oklahoma!* with Oscar Hammerstein II, had produced a revival of *A Connecticut Yankee*—and Larry Hart was dead. The old partnership was ended, and Dick Rodgers was about to enter into a new one. Suppose we turn back now, and trace the career of the new partner.

# Part Two

In Berlin, Germany, the winter of 1862-63 was a severe one, so much so that the Landwehr Canal froze over. On an afternoon in January a sixteen-year-old boy named Oscar Hammerstein played hooky from his violin lesson to go skating, thereby making operatic history in New York. For his father, who had a sense of irony, beat him with a skate strap; whereupon the son, with an equal sense of irony, sold his violin (which must have been an expensive one) and came to America on the proceeds.

The Civil War was on, thousands of men were at the front, and jobs were plentiful. Within a few days after his arrival in New York young Hammerstein had no trouble in getting a job as a cigar maker—a trade of which he was totally ignorant. He must have been an apt student, however, for five years later he invented a cigar-making machine for which the sale of the patent brought him six thousand dollars (equivalent to thirty thousand dollars today). All in all, he took out over a hundred patents, which yielded him a comfortable fortune of about a hundred thousand dollars.

Possessed of this wealth at a comparatively early age, he was free to indulge his twin passions: building and operating theaters, and presenting opera. He began in a modest way by leasing and operating the Stadt Theater on the

Bowery, where he produced three plays of his own, for one of which he wrote music. Incidentally, years later he made a bet with his composer-friend Gustave Kerker that he could write the book, lyrics, and music of a complete operetta in forty-eight hours. Locked in a hotel room for the stipulated two days and nights, he emerged triumphantly with a piece entitled *The Kohinoor*, which was actually—if unsuccessfully—produced.

All in all, Hammerstein built ten theaters and opera houses in New York alone, beginning with the Harlem Opera House, which was erected, according to three eminent authorities, in 1880, 1888, or 1890—take your pick. Others were the Harlem Music Hall, and the Olympia, Republic, and Harris theaters. He also built his first Manhattan Opera House, which was later rechristened Koster and Bial's. The two most famous, still associated with his name, were Hammerstein's Victoria and the second Manhattan Opera House.

The Victoria, at the corner of Seventh Avenue and Forty-second Street (ultimately torn down and replaced by the Rialto), was a fabulously profitable vaudeville theater, managed by Willy Hammerstein, one of Oscar's sons, presenting a bill that reflected the elder Hammerstein's highly individualistic ideas regarding theatrical entertainment. It was at the Victoria that the Empire City Quartet sang "Sweet Adeline" for the first time on any stage, and that Berlin's "Alexander's Ragtime Band" was first unveiled. Will Rogers once rode a pony on its stage. One policy of the house was to include a newspaper headliner in every bill. Anyone who had achieved temporary notoriety for doing no matter what, would probably be booked for a week at the Victoria. There is a legend to the effect that one man approached Oscar (it may have been Willy) with a weird proposal: He would come out on the stage and blow out his brains on condition that Hammerstein give ten thousand dollars to his starving wife and children. They do say that Hammerstein looked thoughtful for a moment, and then inquired, mildly, "Suppose you get an encore?"

The Shooting Showgirls were less apocryphal. They were a pair of theatrical cuties who burst into print by pumping lead into the legs of the elderly admirer of one, or possibly both, of them. After the law had done with them they duly got their week at the Victoria. The quality of their talents is best gauged by Oscar's remark after seeing them: "I wouldn't give them another week if they shot the King of England."

If the New York State Boxing Commission should suddenly announce a season of classic ballet, the news would be somewhat less astounding than Hammerstein's announcement, in 1906, that he was heading an opera company to present grand opera in his newly erected Manhattan Opera House on Thirty-fourth Street. This ex-cigar maker and vaudeville magnate produce opera? Buck the Metropolitan? The consensus was that Hammerstein was mad.

Since this is, after all, supposed to be the story of his grandson's career, it would hardly be appropriate to go into much detail concerning his own. Briefly, he was not mad, but he almost drove the directors of the Metropolitan mad. For four years he gave the fat and complacent Metropolitan such a shaking up as it had not had in a generation. He gave New Yorkers a chance to hear operas, mostly French, some of which had never been heard there—works such as *Louise, Tales of Hoffmann, Herodiade, Sappho, Pelléas et Mélisande,* and *Thaïs.* The list of great artists that he introduced includes Melba, Tetrazzini, Garden, Renaud, Dalmores, Sammarco, McCormack. He produced Strauss's *Elektra* for the first time, and presented *Salome* with Mary Garden doing her own Dance of the Seven Veils.

All this he accomplished in the face of sturdy opposition. He wished, for example, to present Nellie Melba in one of her greatest roles, Mimi, in *La Bohème,* an opera that the Metropolitan regarded as its personal property. Puccini's publishers could not prevent his performing it, provided he paid the customary performance fees, but they could—and did—refuse to sell or rent him the orchestral score and parts. He promptly bought an incomplete set of parts from a traveling opera company that had been stranded in Mexico, and hired some skilled arrangers to fill in the missing parts and reconstruct the score. Then he struck another snag. His chief conductor, the great Cleofonte Campanini, was a Puccini specialist. Somehow, and in some way, it was delicately intimated that if Campanini conducted *La Bohème* for Hammerstein he would never again conduct in Italy. Hammerstein solved that puzzle, too. At the performance, which was a triumph, the conductor's podium was occupied by an honest second-rater named Tanara, while Campanini, standing on the audience side of the rail, without a score, waved a baton, ostensibly for his own entertainment.

There were other obstacles. For one thing, the Manhattan Opera House—now chiefly used to house union meetings—was situated between Eighth and Ninth Avenues, a wild, western region that most New Yorkers had never explored. For another, he lacked a Diamond Horseshoe of solvent and benevolent directors. Mrs. Clarence Mackay (Irving Berlin's mother-in-law) did start a Manhattan Opera Diamond Horseshoe of her own; but Hammerstein, with his talent for insult, managed to pick a quarrel, and they parted. Nevertheless, he kept stubbornly on his way, relying on the general public for support, and making up deficits out of his own pocket.

Early in 1910 he set sail for Europe, whence a stream of cablegrams began to arrive, announcing the forthcoming productions of such and such operas and the engagement of such and such great singers. Meanwhile, in New York, his lawyers were dickering with the Board of the Metropolitan. In April, 1910, the Board and Hammerstein signed an agreement whereby he agreed not to produce opera in the United States for a period of ten years, in return for which he received the sum of one million dollars.

The greatest bluff in the history of music had worked. According to the late Morris Gest, who was at the time a sort of general factotum around the Hammerstein offices, the boss had enough money to buy a ticket to Europe, but not enough, if the deal had fallen through, to get back.

He promptly took his million and went to London, where he built the London Opera House and started production. Considering the fact that Covent Garden, even without competition, had never made money, it was not surprising that the London venture was a failure. He had already built a Metropolitan Opera House in Philadelphia, in 1908. In 1913 he built the Lexington Opera House in New York. He undertook to produce opera in the latter, but was stopped by an injunction obtained by the directors of the Metropolitan, on the ground that he was violating his agreement to keep out of opera until 1920. In 1919 he announced his intention of producing again the following year. Only his death prevented that. His opera house was used for occasional visits from the Chicago-Philadelphia Opera Company. As Loew's Lexington it has long since been a motion picture theater.

With a father who was a theater manager, and a grandfather who was one of the greatest showmen in the world, it is hardly surprising that Oscar Hammerstein II developed an interest in the theater at an early age. Even his uncle, Arthur, after flirting with the masonry and building businesses, eventually turned to producing plays—including some written by his nephew. True, there was family opposition to young Oscar's embracing a theatrical career; but on the whole it was rather halfhearted, confined to words rather than deeds.

Oscar II was born July 12, 1895, in an apartment on New York's upper west side, "somewhere near 135th Street," as he vaguely relates. His first three years are shrouded in obscurity, although it is probably safe to assume that they were tranquil ones. When he was four, the family moved down to an apartment on Madison Avenue, near Mount Morris Park. For reasons that still escape him he was moved still farther down; for while he ate with the family, he lived and slept in the apartment of his maternal grand-father, James Nimmo, on the floor below. Mr. Nimmo, a retired insurance man, and the youngster were close friends. Their morning ritual was unvarying: up at six, then, after a light collation consisting of milk punch and sour balls (a second cousin, I gather, of the lemon drop), off to Mount Morris Park, there to discuss whatever topics are discussed by an old gentleman and a little boy. The park boasted a bell tower, up which an old man clambered every morning at seven sharp, to ring the hour. This was the signal for the two to return home for the more substantial official break-fast. Incidentally, Oscar's paternal grandfather, Oscar the Great, existed more as a presence felt than as an actuality. He never visited the rest of the family, nor did the family visit him. Oscar II saw him no more than half a dozen times in his life.

Strolling in Mount Morris Park with Grandfather Nimmo was not the alpha and omega of existence, however, even to a four-year-old. There was something beyond the horizon, a mysterious something called the Theater, which took his father away every morning, sent him back every night, and provided the family with an endless topic of conversation. This Theater must be something wonderful if it could pos-sess the lives of those about him so completely. He began demanding to be taken to see it. The family reaction to this request was an immediate and emphatic no. His father, in particular, was loud in his opinion that three members of the family in this raffish profession were enough. No son of his . . . etc.

However, the granite persistence of a small boy can be

guaranteed to wear down all but the strongest of adults. It followed, therefore, that upon a certain afternoon young Oscar's harried father took him to a matinee at the Victoria. In the lobby he had one of his rare glimpses of his paternal grandfather, who cast a jaundiced eye upon him and acknowledged the introduction with a cryptic clucking noise. Once inside, he was placed in a stage box while his father left to attend to other business.

The house lights dimmed and the curtain rose. The stage was flooded with golden light, and a group of unearthly beautiful young women were gathered about a golden fish net, which they seemed to be mending as they sang:

> Oh, I am a fisher maiden,
> A child of the water,
> The fisherman's daughter. . . .

His recollection of just what else went on, that enchanted afternoon, is excusably dim. There were lights, and color, and music, and singing, and dancing, all fused together in one magnificent blur. By the end of Part One the theater had one more slave.

Meanwhile, there was the unfinished business of growing up to be attended to. For a while he went to Public School Number Nine, at West End Avenue and Eighty-second Street. At ten, he was entered as a day student at Hamilton Institute. This, like several other boys' schools in New York, was perfunctorily military, and he spent some of his afternoons drilling in the Twenty-second Regiment Armory. In view of his spectacularly nonmilitary stance today, one can't help wondering who his drillmasters were. Summers he spent at the Weingart Institute camp at Highmount (run, by the way, by a school that he did not, at the time, attend). He loved camping, and loved the country—which doubtless explains the deep feeling for nature that is bustin' out all over so many of his lyrics. At twelve he had a short story, "The Adventures of a Penny," printed in the Hamilton *Echo*, and at fifteen edited the Weingart *Review*—the first modest harbingers of his career.

Considering that the overwhelming bulk of his work has been done for the lyric theater, it may come as a mild surprise to learn that he disliked opera from an early age. "Opera," he relates, was practically a dirty word in the vocabulary of his family. This, of course, sprang from the dismay with which the family viewed the eldest Hammerstein's reckless pursuit of the lyric drama. Every time he built a new theater, the same colloquy would take place:

"Is it *just* a theater?"

"Of course it's just a theater!"

Whereupon, on inspecting the new edifice, they would find an orchestra pit worthy of the Metropolitan, and walls plentifully bedecked with busts of Beethoven, Mozart, Wagner, and Verdi—just in case. . . .

During the days of the Manhattan Opera Company (from young Oscar's eleventh to fifteenth years), whenever some financial emergency developed in Thirty-fourth Street, the old gentleman had an exasperating habit of turning up in the box office of the Victoria and scooping up whatever loose cash he needed—literally robbing the till. This particularly embittered the soul of Willy Hammerstein, who liked everything to be business-like.

In 1912, when Oscar II was seventeen, he entered Columbia University in the class of 1916. The English Department at Columbia in those days was a brilliant one, headed by Brander Matthews and including John Erskine and Carl Van Doren. This may partly explain why the roster of undergraduates of that era contained so many names—besides his own—destined later to be famous ones in the field of letters: names such as Howard Dietz, public relations expert, lyrist,[1] and playwright; Bennett Cerf, the publisher; Morrie Ryskind, librettist; M. Lincoln Schuster and Richard L. Simon, two other publishers; and Lorenz Hart, Richard Rodgers' partner-to-be.

In the spring of his freshman year young Hammerstein played baseball on the freshman team, but never succeeded in making the varsity. He confides that he was consequently considerably surprised, upon meeting Andy Coakley, the Columbia baseball coach, a year after his graduation, to hear him remark, "Gee, Oscar, I wish you were back. I could certainly use a good first baseman!"

But belles-lettres and baseball were not his main ambition at Columbia. That was, in his own words, "the varsity show. It was put on every spring, and ran a week in the Astor ballroom. What better reason for going to Columbia?" If you will turn back to page 10 you will discover that Rodgers and Hammerstein not only think alike, but express themselves almost incredibly alike . . . or did they rehearse that bit?

Unlike Rodgers, however, young Hammerstein had a twofold ambition. He wanted not only to write but to act;

[1] See footnote on page 61.

and his second wish was granted first. In 1915, his junior year, he was awarded the second comedy part in the then current varsity show, *On Your Way*.

Willy Hammerstein had died the year before. It has been alleged that Oscar's father exacted a deathbed promise from Arthur Hammerstein that he would keep his son out of the theater. Oscar doubts this, being of the opinion that if it were true he would have heard of it at the time. One request Willy Hammerstein did make. Ignoring the fact that tobacco had been the foundation of the family fortunes, he asked Oscar not to smoke. And Oscar never has. "He was not an exacting father," he says, "and I wouldn't have liked to displease him. If he really had asked my uncle to keep me out of the theater, I might have tried."

As a matter of fact, he did try. When his uncle voiced considerably less than complete approval of his preoccupation with varsity shows, the nephew pointed out that, after all, these were mere extramural activities, and announced that he intended to study law.

Meanwhile, he must have been doing some serious work, for in that same junior year Carl Van Doren, who was his faculty adviser, sent for him and asked what he planned to do after graduation. Oscar again announced that he was going to be a lawyer. Van Doren made a face. "Oh . . . well . . . in that case . . . I thought you might be going to write."

"This," says Hammerstein, "is precisely what I was dying to hear somebody say. I left his office and floated down Morningside Drive."

Which did not prevent his enrolling in Columbia Law School in what would have been his senior year at college.

*103*

He received his B.A. at the end of the year, first-year law being counted toward his arts degree. The outstanding event of the year, however—in his opinion at least—was the fact that he played a comedy part in the 1916 varsity show, *The Peace Pirates,* by Herman Mankiewicz, in which he appeared modestly clad in a leopard skin. In his second year at law school he not only wrote the varsity show, *Home, James,* with Herman Axelrod (now in real estate), but also played the leading comedy role, assigned to him by the indulgent librettist, and sang and danced.

Altogether, 1917 was an eventful year. Still in law school, he took a part-time job with the law firm of Blumenstiel and Blumenstiel, who, in a moment of inadvertence, undertook to use him as a process server. He was not a howling success at process serving, since he would have been an admirable model for Webster's comic strip, "The Timid Soul." He would ring a prospective victim's doorbell, and upon being informed that the gentleman was out, would apologize and trustfully depart. Entering a saloon and asking for the proprietor, he would encounter blank ignorance on the part of the customers as to the proprietor's name or whereabouts.

Blumenstiel and Blumenstiel assigned him to indoor work, which it appears could not have been particularly congenial, since he tried to enlist in the Army. He was rejected as underweight, a fact that is of twofold interest: first, that the Army was concerned with weight in those days; second, that the present-day Oscar Hammerstein II (not that he is exactly corpulent) could ever have been underweight.

As has happened to other men, it was a young woman who supplied the impetus that started him on his life's work. Her name was Myra Finn, and she was a distant relative of Dr. William Rodgers (*q.v.*) The two young people met at a house party at Deal Beach, New Jersey, promptly fell in love, and decided to be married. But there was one obstacle: money. Oscar's father had left him some securities that brought him about fifty dollars a week; but that sum, even when augmented by the five dollars a week that Blumenstiel and Blumenstiel were paying him, could hardly be described as princely, even in those days. So he appealed to Arthur Hammerstein for a job—any job.

Uncle Arthur was inclined to be unco-operative, partly because his nephew was proposing to throw away two years of legal education, and partly because two generations in show business were enough. His nephew countered by pointing out that if two generations were in show business, didn't that indicate that show business was in the blood of the Hammersteins? Why not, at least, give him a chance to find out? The nephew won. Not without audible misgivings, Arthur Hammerstein gave him the job of assistant stage manager of a current production of his, *You're in Love*, at twenty dollars a week. Accordingly in the summer of 1917, Oscar Hammerstein and Myra Finn were married.

With the closing of *You're in Love* young Hammerstein received a promotion to full stage manager of *Sometime*, a musical comedy by Rida Johnson Young, based on a scenario by Oscar II. The cast included Ed Wynn and Mae West. Hammerstein still remembers the first reading of the book. Wynn was playing the principal comedy role, a character named Loney. The opening scene, designed to build up his entrance, was studded with references to "dear old Loney," "sweet old Loney," "darling old Loney," and the like. Wynn listened with increasing exasperation, and finally burst forth irritably: "Want me to be funny? Then for God's sake say, 'Where is that louse Loney, that stinker Loney, that crook Loney?'! Then, when I come on, they'll laugh." Oscar II says it was his first lesson in writing comedy.

Mae West took a fancy to the young stage manager, and proclaimed him her mascot, insisting that he be in the wings whenever she went on. One day she took him aside, and said, "Kid, get out of the theater and be a lawyer. As long as you've studied law, be one. The theater isn't for you. You've got too much class"—advice that was not as fantastic as it sounds today. Thirty-odd years ago there was still a considerable gulf between show people and nonprofessionals. Actors, to many laymen, were still rogues and mountebanks. If an actor could remark, carelessly, "Friends of mine out in front tonight. No, not show people. In the steel business," he would be treated with enhanced respect by the rest of the cast.

However, class or no class, Oscar II had no intention of going back to the law. His world was the theater; the only question being, what part of the theater? Despite his cavortings in varsity shows, he had no serious ambition to be an actor. He certainly didn't want to be a stage manager; and the careers of his grandfather and father had given him no managerial aspirations. Perhaps Carl Van Doren was right. Perhaps he could *write* for the theater. He turned to his uncle for advice.

It so happened that Arthur Hammerstein had read a story about a girl who broke away from a tyrannical family, fled a loveless marriage, went through many vicissitudes, including working in a gambling house, and finally wed her own true love. He suggested that Oscar try his hand at making a play out of it—if he liked it. "I would have liked the telephone book if it would get me a production," says Oscar II. He resigned from his job as stage manager and set to work. The play, entitled *The Light*, was put into production by his uncle (his grandfather attended the dress rehearsal) and opened in New Haven on Wednesday evening, May 21, 1919.

The verdict of the local critics was prompt and cataclysmic. The *New Haven* minced no words: "Back to the darkness from which it emerged for cradling last evening will soon go 'The Light,' a play by Oscar Hammerstein II produced by Uncle Arthur. Its christening robe may well suffice as a shroud for a deadly dull play." The *Courier Journal* cryptically remarked that "if you are fond of this sort of performance you will find the play . . . mildly interesting," but did grudgingly admit that the author "has pictured some types that are alarmingly true to life."

*The Light* lasted five performances. "I have always liked myself," observes the author, "for my attitude toward that play. When I went into the Saturday matinee I knew I had a big flop. There must have been about twenty people in the house. When the ingénue came on, one of her lines was, 'Everything is falling down around me'—and at that precise moment her petticoat started falling down. I didn't wait for the yell that followed. I just ran out of the theater, went to the park, and sat on a bench. While I was sitting there, an idea came to me for a new show. So I started writing it."

The "new show" was a musical comedy for which Herbert Stothart provided the music, Oscar II being responsible for both book and lyrics. The Actors' Equity strike of 1919, which created such chaos in the theatrical world for a time, was indirectly a boon to the authors. Although he had resigned from his stage manager job, Oscar II had been assigned to the task of readying the road companies of some of his uncle's productions. Came the strike, and there were no road companies, leaving him ample time to work on his script.

The new piece, produced by Uncle Arthur, opened at the Central Theatre in New York on January 5, 1920. The plot—which the author readily concedes to have possessed certain overtones of *Madame Butterfly*—concerned a soldier of the A.E.F. who went to France and fell in love with a French girl. Returning to the United States, he became engaged to a former American sweetheart. Later he returned to France and the arms of his Gallic love. It opened on the road under the title of *Joan of Arkansas*, which aroused the prompt disapproval of the clergy. It was obligingly retitled *Toinette*. This was objected to in certain squeamish quarters as sounding too much like "toilet." Accordingly it made its New York bow under the harmless cognomen of *Always You*.

The New York critics received the offering with mixed emotions. The *Times* hailed it as being "full of melody, jazz, girls, and comedy, all of the right kind [whatever that might mean]. Also the lyrics are more clever than those of the average musical comedy." The *Globe* averred that both the author and the composer "have done far above the ordinary. . . . Delightfully staged, the music is tuneful, the book above par." The *World*, however, dismissed it as "a musical comedy for the tired businessman," while the *Tribune* announced that "of the three [who was the third?] Mr. Stothart is the only one deserving of any congratulations."

*Always You* had a New York run—or is "amble" the word?—of sixty-six performances. To be sure that was sixty-one more than *The Light* had enjoyed, and it spent a respectable six months on the road. Still, its career left something to be desired.

The desired something was provided by a new Arthur Hammerstein production, which opened in New York a few days before *Always You* finished its road tour. Its title was *Tickle Me*. It was an unabashed vehicle for Frank Tinney, the vaudeville and revue star, with a book and lyrics that had engaged the combined efforts of Otto Harbach, Frank Mandel, and Oscar II, with Herbert Stothart again providing the music. The "story"—to coin a phrase—concerned Frank Tinney, who, in the role of Frank Tinney, accompanied a motion picture company to Tibet, where he played several parts before the camera and several more before the footlights, while the scenery was being changed. Also, as a toxicologist might phrase it, "of subsidiary love interest, a trace."

One feature of the production was a "ground glass" effect devised by Arthur Hammerstein. The younger Hammerstein is a little vague as to what it was and how it worked; but apparently it was some sort of arrangement of successive gauze curtains, through which the actors walked into a fadeout. It was an ingenious idea, its only flaw being that it didn't work. On the opening night of the tryout in Long Branch, New Jersey, Mr. Tinney came before the footlights and spake, in substance, as follows:

"This next scene won't work, so you won't see it. I just wanted you to know that the boy and girl do get together. So now you can go home."

Which they did. After some frenzied carpentering including writing a whole new second act in twenty-four hours, *Tickle Me* opened at the Selwyn Theatre on August 17, 1920.

The New York critics came through handsomely. Barring one sour note sounded by the *World*—"Little to distinguish it . . . suffered through lack of comedians" (that must have pleased Tinney!)—the others—the *Sun*, the *Globe*, the *Telegram*, the *Telegraph*—agreed that *Tickle Me* was "a lavish and pleasing performance" . . . "a joyous, romping absurdity" . . . "a riot of fun" . . . and other pleasing things.

*Tickle Me* was definitely "in." It ran for seven months in New York, with an additional, profitable road tour. Oscar II was tasting the heady wine—and ready cash—of success.

But as Solomon was once heard to remark, wine is a mocker. The Hammerstein record was destined to register four errors before another hit. First came *Jimmie*, which told the tale of the long-lost daughter of a millionaire who is brought up in ignorance of her true station, but is finally —ever hear *Mignon* at the Metropolitan? Otto Harbach and Frank Mandel joined forces on the book, with lyrics by Oscar II and music by Herbert Stothart. Arthur Hammerstein presented it at the newly built Apollo Theatre on November 17, 1920. The critics were kind. "Amusement loving New York is happy enough when it peeks into a splendid new theatre . . . but it rejoices in being presented on the same night to a musical production like 'Jimmie.' " Thus the *World*'s reviewer, fairly representative of the critical consensus. Amusement-loving New York, however, was less cordial, and voted thumbs down after nine weeks.

Nothing daunted, the team of Mandel and Hammerstein went to work on a play for O. P. Heggie, entitled *Pop*. Details as to its production are missing, save for the fact that Al H. Woods did produce it, in the fall of 1921, and that—in the words of Oscar II—"I loved it. Nobody else did."

*Pop* having been laid to rest, Hammerstein promptly went to work on a new musical comedy, writing all the lyrics and sharing the book with Guy Bolton, with music by the practically permanent Herbert Stothart. The plot was understandably vague, in view of the fact that Frank Tinney headed the cast, playing Frank Tinney. Entitled *Daffy Dill*, it was unveiled by Arthur Hammerstein at the Apollo Theatre on August 14, 1922. The critical verdicts ranged from the *Telegram*'s "two and a half hours of pure joy" to the *Times*'s "a somewhat hybrid entertainment. . . . The plot is terrible." The piece had the melancholy satisfaction

*111*

of enjoying (if you can call it that) precisely the same run —nine weeks—as the ill-fated *Jimmie*.

Bloody but unbowed, our hero called in Frank Mandel and went to work, the result of their labors being *Queen o' Hearts* which was presented by Max Spiegal at the George M. Cohan Theatre on October 10, 1922, eleven days before the closing of *Daffy Dill*. There were two composers, Lewis Gensler and Dudley Wilkinson. The star was Nora Bayes, and the cast included two of her protégés: a promising young girl named Norma Terris and a hitherto unknown young entertainer named Harry Richman— which would indicate that Miss Bayes was no mean picker of talent. The reviews were unanimous: "Pretty chorus, some good tunes . . . sparkling, jingling . . . goes with a bang . . . capitally done." The year was at the spring, so to speak, and all was definitely right with the world.

But the last word belongs, not to Browning, but to Irving Berlin: There is *no* business like show business. *Queen o' Hearts* closed after thirty-nine performances.

Of the seven stage pieces that young Hammerstein had written up to then, five had been produced by Arthur Hammerstein. Of these five, one could be called a hit—albeit a mild one. The others were failures, their four sets of scenery, props, and costumes achieving a combined New York run of 213 performances, only six more than the run of *Tickle Me*, the hit. So far, his investment in Oscar II had been a losing one.

But Uncle Arthur's faith in his nephew's talents was vindicated and rewarded with his production of *Wildflower* at the Casino Theatre on February 7, 1923. The book and lyrics were by Harbach and the twenty-eight-year-old Hammerstein, with a score shared by Herbert Stothart and Vincent Youmans, and the cast was headed by Edith Day and Guy Robertson. The plot, concerning an Italian damsel who will inherit millions if she can keep her temper for six months, was not exactly epic, but with good lyrics and a charming score it sufficed.

The reviewers called it all sorts of pretty names: "A musical of delightful manner and really gorgeous melodies" (Quinn Martin in the *World*); "an adroit and workmanlike example of the genus musical comedy, turned out by two veterans in their line" (the *Times*); "plenty of catchy and tuneful music, much pep, some good dancing, attractive and colorful costumes" (*Evening Mail*). Only Alexander Woollcott, in the *Herald*, was a bit on the lukewarm side: "It is an entirely unobjectionable mixture of songs and dances which we are going to have a mighty hard time remembering." But despite Alec's lack of co-operation the public insisted on whistling "Wildflower" and "Bambalina." The piece ran for fifteen months in New York and sent two companies on the road.

Incidentally, *Wildflower* marked the beginning of a curious cycle of ups and downs in Hammerstein's career. Every year, for the ensuing six years—that is, from 1923 through 1928—he turned out one musical comedy that ran a year or more in New York, and one or two that were comparative failures; or, as he puts it, "home runs and strike-outs." The strike-out—or, shall we say, out-at-second —for 1923 was presented by Arthur Hammerstein at the Imperial Theatre on Christmas night of that year. William

Cary Duncan and Oscar II wrote the book and lyrics, with a score by Vincent Youmans and the inevitable Herbert Stothart. They called it *Plain Jane* originally, only to make the uncomfortable discovery that not only was that the title of another play, by Jack Hazzard, the comedian, but also that the plot bore a strong family resemblance to that of the Hazzard show. After five weeks of rewriting on the road, it came to New York as *Mary Jane McKane*, with Mary Hay in the title role. The critics were enthusiastic, the public only mildly so. *Mary Jane McKane* was not a disaster—it did run nineteen weeks—but it was by no means a hit.

The dawn of 1924 was not particularly rosy, either. Milton Herbert Gropper had written a play called *Gypsy Jim*, all about an eccentric millionaire who went about restoring people's faith in themselves, and had called Hammerstein in to administer the final polish to the script. Arthur Hammerstein produced it at the Forty-ninth Street Theatre on January 14, 1924. The dialogue was a trifle on the flowery side, which caused Alexander Woollcott to remark, in the *World*:

This lyric speech became so contagious that the authors were in grave danger of seeing the newspapers break out this morning in a rash of notices such as this:
> Oscar Hammerstein 2d and Milton Gropper
> Wrote a comedy that came an awful cropper.

Not much, that, as poetry, but fairly prophetic. *Gypsy Jim* passed away quietly after a run of thirty-nine performances.

The gloom deepened. The next to feel the ax was *New Toys*, another Gropper-Hammerstein play dealing with the second year of marriage. Trailing the rather lengthy subtitle, "A Comic Tragedy of Married Life after the Baby Arrives," it was presented at the Fulton Theatre by Sam H. Harris on February 18, 1924. According to Percy Hammond of the *Tribune*, its principal faults were those of "immaturity, technical inexperience, and general unintelligence," sharing the *coup de grâce* with John Corbin, who observed in the *Times* that "perhaps the real fault with 'New Toys' is that with all its surface pretence of realism, it is plain buncombe through and through." That settled it. *New Toys* lasted the length of most new toys: three weeks.

Oddly enough, although this was Hammerstein's worst failure, it was the first work of his to be made into a motion picture. First National presented it in 1925, with a cast that included Richard Barthelmess, Mary Hay, and Clifton Webb.

The wheel of '24 was due to take a turn—and it did. On the evening of September 2, 1924, Arthur Hammerstein presented *Rose Marie* at the Imperial Theatre; book and lyrics by Otto Harbach and Oscar II, music by Herbert Stothart and Rudolf Friml. The plot was simplicity itself: Heroine loves Hero, is desired by Villain; Hero accused of murder; Villain gives Heroine choice of giving Hero up to police or marrying Villain; Heroine agrees to marry Villain; Hero freed, Heroine gets out of promise. Dennis King and Mary Ellis headed the cast.

It is safe to assume that Arthur Hammerstein passed a

nervous evening at the opening. The average theatrical producer today is less an entrepreneur than a promoter, his main efforts being directed toward finding financial backers. Hammerstein, like many other producers in those days, used his own money. *Rose Marie* represented a primary investment of $83,000, plus an additional $2,400 that Charles Lemaire, the costume designer, had inveigled out of him for a number involving girls dressed as totem poles—a grand total of $85,400. That was no mean sum for even a prosperous producer to risk.

His worries probably lessened as the evening wore on. The story, simple as it was, successfully held the audience, the two principals were brilliant, and Friml's contributions to the score were among his best. More than a quarter-century later, three of them—"Rose Marie," "Indian Love Call," and "Totem Tom Tom"—still haunt the airwaves.

He must have been still further reassured the next morning, when he read the papers: "One of the big musical successes of the season" (*Times*); "one of the best mixtures of music and drama" (*World*); "a production with haunting melodies, a thrilling plot, clever comedy, and unusual novelties" (*Mirror*); "the bon voyage basket of musical shows . . . a beautiful composite photograph of a three-ring circus" (*Tribune*).

*Rose Marie* stayed at the Imperial until the middle of January, 1926—one year, four months, and seven days —a record-breaking run for its times, exceeded only by that of *Show Boat* three years later (and then only by fifteen days). It had a brief revival at the Century in 1927. Meanwhile, four *Rose Marie* companies had gone on the road. It had a highly successful run in London, and was twice made into a picture by M-G-M: as a silent, in 1928, starring Joan Crawford, and as a musical, in 1936, for Jeanette MacDonald and Nelson Eddy. It is still a stock company favorite.

Early in 1925 the younger Hammerstein had gone to London to supervise the English production. From there he went to Paris, where he worked on the outline of a new book. On his return home, however, he found that Otto Harbach also had an idea for a new show, and also a new composer (new to Hammerstein, that is), Jerome Kern. Shelving the Hammerstein outline for the moment, the trio went to work on the Harbach plan. The fruit of their labors was *Sunny*, produced by Charles Dillingham at the New Amsterdam Theatre on September 22, 1925. Its story was that of a circus girl who loves one man, is loved by another, and marries, divorces, and remarries a third.

Dillingham gave it a glittering cast, headed by Marilyn Miller and Jack Donahue, and including Joseph Cawthorn, Clifton Webb, Mary Hay, and Borrah Minevitch, the Harmonica Rascal, who had a solo number. Like most Dillingham productions, it had plenty of dancing. Kern's score included two popular classics, "Sunny" and "Who?" The public clasped the show to its bosom, and it ran for over a year. In the fall of 1926 an English company produced it at the London Hippodrome, where it ran for eleven months. In 1930, First National made a silent picture of it, and in 1941 R.K.O. issued it as a musical. Hammerstein says that he never did like it.

*Sunny* was Hammerstein's twelfth stage work. Nine of

the twelve were musical comedies, for which, either as
sole author or as collaborator, he had written 150 song
lyrics. Just six of these were hits—a batting average of
.040. Yet this painfully meager percentage is significant
only as it illustrates the heavy handicap under which any
lyrist labors. Let's put it in equation form:

Brilliant Score + Brilliant Lyrics = Success
Brilliant Score + Dull Lyrics     = Success
Dull Score      + Brilliant Lyrics = Failure

In other words, the lyric has much less to do with the
making of a song hit than does the music. Given a first-
rate lyric and a first-rate tune, each enhances the other
(*Pal Joey* and *South Pacific*, for instance). But a brilliant
tune can become a hit in spite of the lyric. Take, for example, Arthur Schwartz's "Dancing in the Dark," which
has been a favorite for years. Yet I defy even Howard
Dietz, who wrote the lyric, to tell me precisely what it
means. On the other hand, the most brilliant lyrics ever
written, accompanied by a dull tune, cannot make it a hit.
People find music easier to remember than words. Besides,
the tune of a popular song is much more frequently *played*
(in night clubs, dance halls, in radio and television) than
it is *sung*; so that, in the last analysis, the lyrist is at the
mercy of the composer.

Hammerstein's six song hits were the work of three
extremely popular composers: "Bambalina" and "Wild
Flower," by Youmans; "Rose Marie" and "Indian Love
Call" by Friml; and "Sunny" and "Who?" by Kern. Most
of his other songs had been written with Herbert Stothart,
who could provide a good, solid, workman-like score—

what is known as a good "show score"—but couldn't manage hit tunes. All of which left Oscar II more to be pitied than scorned.

Incidentally, this theory of mine has been vociferously assailed by Mr. Billy Rose, who maintains that many a Hit Parade song owes its popularity as much to the lyric as to the tune—sometimes more so; and cites such "pop" songs as "I Found a Million-Dollar Baby in a Five-and-Ten-Cent Store," "It's Only a Paper Moon," and "I've Got a Feeling I'm Falling" to prove his point (they all happen to be Mr. Rose's lyrics). In his field Mr. Rose may be right. On the other hand, the so-called "production" writer, the man who writes lyrics for a musical comedy, has to turn out, not one isolated song lyric, but from sixteen to eighteen; and while one or two of his lyrics may top the music in importance, there still remain fifteen or so, the music for which must be at least adequate if the show is to have any hope of success. I still believe that—at least in the musical comedy field:

Brilliant lyrics + Dull Score = Failure

Three months after *Sunny* had begun its prosperous run—that is, on December 30, 1925—Arthur Hammerstein presented *A Song of the Flame* at New York's Forty-fourth Street Theatre. This was the story on which Hammerstein had been working in Paris, earlier in the year. Harbach had collaborated on the book and lyrics, with a score by Herbert Stothart and George Gershwin. There was scenery by Joseph Urban and a cast of two hundred. The auspices seemed favorable. But the fatal home-run-strike-out cycle—otherwise known as Hammerstein's Disease—did its dirty work. One hit for '25 was enough. *A Song of the Flame* was not a disaster, but it was anything but a hit. Its run of six months was not enough to pay for the production.

*The Wild Rose*, with a book by Harbach and Hammerstein and a score by Rudolf Friml, which Arthur Hammerstein presented at the Martin Beck Theatre on November 1, 1926, was even less successful. The critics did their best—"spirited and charming musical comedy" . . . "typical of the good taste and opulent decoration that are Arthur Hammerstein's trademarks" . . . "a gorgeous musical show" . . . "well sung, handsomely mounted"—but to no avail. *The Wild Rose* wilted after a run of eight weeks.

Remember, though, that Hammerstein's Disease works two ways. Having had his strike-out for 1926, he was due for a home run. It arrived just twenty-nine days after the debut of *The Wild Rose*, when, on November 30, Schwab and Mandel produced *The Desert Song* at the Casino Theatre. Frank Mandel collaborated with the familiar Harbach-Hammerstein team in concocting the book and lyrics, with Sigmund Romberg providing the twenty-six numbers that made up the score.

The revolt of the Riffs, under the leadership of Abdel Krim, against the French protectorate in Morocco, had been very much in the news during 1925-26, and the authors of *The Desert Song* promptly snatched it out of the headlines to put it on the stage. The plot concerns the slightly schizophrenic son (Robert Halliday) of the governor of a French Moroccan province (Edmund Elton), who poses by day as an amiable fathead and sallies forth by night to be a Riff leader known as the Red Shadow. He falls in love with a young woman (Vivienne Segal) whose scorn of the wastrel turns to love when she learns that he and the Red Shadow are one.

In view of the subsequent fortunes of *The Desert Song*, its critical reception was oddly mixed. The New York *Sun*, for instance, noted, "Pageantry, romance, ringing music, vitality and humor—that's 'The Desert Song.' What more do you want?" Bide Dudley, in the *Evening World*, proclaimed it "a big, red-blooded, musical treat. It should remain a year—maybe two." On the other hand, according to Richard Watts, Jr., in the *Herald Tribune*, "The question of how simple-minded the book of a musical comedy can be was debated last night, and the verdict arrived at was 'no end.' With the exception of one song, called 'It,' the lyrics gave indication that W. S. Gilbert lived and died in vain."

While Bide Dudley's prediction was not fulfilled to the letter, it came close. *The Desert Song* ran well over a year in New York and had an impressive run at the Drury Lane Theatre in London. Ten years later it had a second run in London and in Sydney, Australia. In 1939 London saw it for the third time; it made its bow that year in Cremorne, Australia. In a tabloid version it traveled the Fanchon and Marco vaudeville circuit for over a year. Since 1932 it has had countless revivals throughout the country. Warners made a Vitaphone picture of it in 1929, and another, with a new story replete with Nazis, in 1943.

All in all, it made a fortune for its creators—and is still contributing.

Exactly a year, to the day, after the opening of *The Desert Song*, Arthur Hammerstein presented *Golden Dawn* at his own theater. Harbach and Hammerstein were, in accordance with standard practice, the coauthors, with the faithful Herbert Stothart sharing the score with Emmerrich Kalman. The plot sounds a little mystifying. According to the official synopsis, it related that "Dawn, supposedly a young and beautiful native [of what?], is brought up by her native nurse, Mooda, to believe she is the destined princess of an African tribe. Along comes Steve Allen, war prisoner of Germany [which war?], to make love to Dawn and unfit her for the princess job. Shep Keyes, a big black, seeks to keep Dawn in the tribe, but Steve finds a way." Louise Hunter, a refugee from the Metropolitan Opera, headed a cast that included another ex-opera diva, Marguerite Sylva, and one Archie Leach, better known today as Cary Grant. The score, by the way, had the distinction of being written, at least in part, by correspondence. Kalman, sojourning in Vienna, was unwilling to come to America to compose his share of the songs. Accordingly, he mailed his tunes to Hammerstein, who dutifully wrote lyrics for them. The piece ran for six months—which was not enough to make it profitable.

In the spring of 1927 Hammerstein had had an excited telephone call from Jerome Kern: "Oscar? I want us to do a show from a book I haven't finished reading. It's by Edna Ferber, and it has a million-dollar title: *Show Boat*."

Hammerstein read the novel and was as enthusiastic as

Kern over its possibilities as a musical comedy. The latter thereupon went into action, cajoling Miss Ferber into letting them have the rights and persuading Florenz Ziegfeld to produce the piece—when it was finished. Then came the problem of turning the novel into a libretto. As the preliminary step the two agreed that each would write his own synopsis of the scenes. When the two versions were compared, they turned out to be virtually identical. And so to work. . . .

Ziegfeld opened *Show Boat* on November 15, 1927, at the National Theatre in Washington, for a two-week tryout. From there it went to the Erlanger Theatre in Philadelphia for a further three weeks. He presented it in New York, at the Ziegfeld Theatre, on the night of December 27, 1927.

*Show Boat* has been so widely read as a novel, and has been seen by so many millions either "live" or as a picture, and has been revived so many times, that its story hardly needs retelling. However, for the sake of the record, be it briefly noted that Cap'n Andy Hawks and his wife, Parthy Ann, have their troubles in bringing up their daughter, Magnolia, on their show boat "Cotton Blossom." Eventually she runs off to marry Gaylord Ravenal, a handsome young gambler. After many vicissitudes, including Gaylord's desertion of Magnolia and their daughter, Kim, the Hawks and Ravenal families are reunited.

The cast was fabulous: Edna May Oliver (Parthy Ann); Charles Winninger (Cap'n Andy); Helen Morgan (Julie); Howard Marsh (Ravenal); Norma Terris (Magnolia); Jules Bledsoe—no one who ever saw and heard them will soon forget them. Of the twenty-four numbers in the score, at least six have become classics of their kind: "Only Make Believe," "Can't Help Lovin' That Man," "You Are Love," "Why Do I Love You?" "Bill," and of course the unforgettable "Ol' Man River."

By a not particularly interesting coincidence, the year that *Show Boat* opened, 1927, marked the one hundredth anniversary of the abolition of slavery in New York State. It may have been remembrance of this interesting fact that inspired some of Hammerstein's Left Wing friends to congratulate him upon his courage in thus voicing the sorrows of an oppressed race. His own explanation of the genesis of "Ol' Man River" is more prosaic. "I needed a song at a certain spot in the first act, and there was nothing in the story to justify a 'situation' number. So I decided to write something about the Mississippi River." (He admits, however, that he may have had an unconscious impulse to write that kind of song.) As it turned out, "Ol' Man River" became practically the theme song of the entire operetta, and has since achieved the dignity of being accepted as a familiar recital number.

The life span of *Show Boat* has been a long one. It stayed at the Ziegfeld Theatre for 572 performances—a year and five months. In 1938 it was seen at the Liverpool Empire, London Royal and Drury Lane theaters. In 1929 Universal released it as a part-talking picture with songs. Laura La Plante was Magnolia, with Joseph Schildkraut as Ravenal and Otis Harlan as Cap'n Andy. Preceding the film, during the New York presentation, Helen Morgan and Jules Bledsoe sang.

In 1932 Ziegfeld revived it at the Casino in New York, for a run of twenty-two weeks with the original cast, except for Paul Robeson, replacing Jules Bledsoe, and Dennis King, replacing Howard Marsh. In 1936 Universal again made a film of it, with Charles Winninger, Paul Robeson, and Helen Morgan playing their original roles. Irene Dunne was Magnolia, Allan Jones was Ravenal, and Helen Westley was Parthy. Hammerstein and Kern supplied two new songs for the picture: "'I Have the Room above Her" and "Ah Still Suits Me."

Ten years later, on January 7, 1946, Kern and Hammerstein revived *Show Boat* again at the Ziegfeld Theatre with an entirely new cast: Ralph Dumke as Cap'n Andy; Ethel Owen as Parthy Ann; Carol Bruce as Julie; Kenneth Spencer as Joe; and Jan Clayton as Magnolia.[2] During the season of 1947-48 Rodgers and Hammerstein presented it on the road, ending with a two-week engagement at the City Center Theatre in New York.[3] In 1951 M-G-M made a film of *Show Boat*, with Kathryn Grayson as Magnolia; Ava Gardner as Julie; Howard Keel as Ravenal; Joe E. Brown as Cap'n Andy; William Warfield as Joe; and Agnes Moorehead as Parthy Ann. For some obscure reason, Charles K. Harris' ancient ballad, "After the Ball," was included in the score.

*Show Boat* was a landmark in more ways than one. It revealed Hammerstein as a master hand at adaptation. It

[2] You may get a faint idea of how production costs have skyrocketed during the past ten years from the fact that after a run of well over a year, playing to capacity houses, this revival had not returned its investment.

[3] It was during the rehearsals of this revival that Jerome Kern died.

is not easy to turn a full-length novel into about three hours of words and music and still retain the flavor and the values of the original. He accomplished it perfectly. Compared with its predecessors, the book of *Show Boat* is not a musical comedy at all. At moments it has overtones of tragedy; at others, it is not afraid to mention the forbidden subject of race prejudice. Its people are real people, and their emotions are real. It is a romance, but it is not a fairy tale.

*Golden Dawn* and *Show Boat* were not the only fruits of the eventful year of 1927. On December 22, five days before the opening of *Show Boat*, Schwab and Mandel produced *New Moon* for a two-weeks' tryout at the Chestnut Street Opera House in Philadelphia. Book and lyrics were the work of Laurence Schwab, Frank Mandel, and Oscar Hammerstein II, with music by Sigmund Romberg. The verdict of the public seems to have been summed up by the Philadelphia matron, who, leaving after the opening performance, was heard to remark, "Well! they'll never fix *that* one in a hundred years." It took something less than a hundred years, as we shall see in due time.

Meanwhile, Hammerstein and Kern started work on a project that they had been considering for some time, a musical version of Don Byrne's novel, *Messer Marco Polo*. They had an option on the stage rights, which they renewed from time to time; but try as they would, and engrossing as the story was, they simply could not manage to concoct the stage version long enough to fill an evening. Padding the plot, they decided, would merely prolong the show at the expense of the dramatic interest. They finally abandoned the enterprise.

During a visit to Berlin, Hammerstein had seen a production called *The Good Soldier Schweik* after a comic-strip character resembling our own Sad Sack. He was fascinated, not so much by the show itself as by the novel mechanics of the production, which included treadmills and scenery projected on the back drops from the rear.

Arrived home, he enthusiastically set to work putting together a show that would allow the new gadgets to do their stuff. The result of his labors was *Good Boy*, which Arthur Hammerstein produced at his own theater on September 5, 1928. The list of collaborators resembled a small directory: Book by Otto Harbach, Oscar II, and Bert Kalmar; music by Harry Ruby and Herbert Stothart. The three librettists must have given themselves stern orders to keep the plot simple—possibly so as not to get in the way of the scenery and treadmills. This is it: Country boy comes to big city, marries actress, loses her, makes a fortune, gets her back. End of plot.

End of show, also, as it turned out. *Good Boy* had a respectable New York run of eight months—which was not enough to pay for the gadgets.

Along what is roughly called "Broadway" it is generally conceded that trying to restage and re-present a show that has flopped is a good deal like trying to win a ball game in the ninth inning with the score 40-0 in favor of the other side. It *can* be done, but it probably won't be. The authors and producers of *New Moon* did it. After the disastrous opening two weeks in Philadelphia it was what is delicately called "closed for revisions"—which generally signifies a one-way trip to the warehouse. In this case, however, they elected to gamble. Hammerstein and Romberg, as well as Schwab and Mandel, had put money into the show for a total investment of a hundred thousand dollars. At the risk of sending good money after bad, they contributed an additional thirty thousand dollars, put *New Moon* through an intensive course of play-doctoring, and opened at the Imperial Theatre in New York on the evening of September 19, 1928.

The cast, headed by Robert Halliday and Evelyn Herbert, unfolded the tale of a young French nobleman (the year is 1788) who is wanted by the Paris police and escapes by becoming a bondservant to a wealthy New Orleans shipowner. He falls in love with his patron's daughter. The police finally track him down and bundle him aboard a ship bound for France. The girl, Marianne, is on the same ship. There is mutiny aboard, the bondservants become masters, and everyone goes ashore to found a new republic (I don't *know* where it is). Marianne, her pride hurt, refuses to marry the young noble. By the end of the evening he has persuaded her.

Granted that this story had moments that took a deal of believing, it added up to a satisfying romantic melodrama, with Romberg and Hammerstein in one of their happiest moods. At least four of the twenty musical numbers—"Softly, as in a Morning Sunrise," "Stout-Hearted Men," "One Kiss," and "Lover, Come Back to Me"—are still with us.

The critics were unanimous in voting yes. Particularly interesting was the verdict of the usually caustic St. John Ervine, the British guest critic of the New York *World*:

The most charming and fragrant entertainment of its sort that
I have seen for a long time. . . . Has taste and distinction . . .
an intelligent story. . . . Not a piece of immortal literature, but
neither is it, as a majority of stories in musical pieces are, a
piece of pure imbecility. . . . See "New Moon" without any
delay.

The public delayed not, and saw it to the tune of a New
York run of a year and three months, a long road tour,
and a successful London production at the Drury Lane
Theatre. M-G-M made a picture of it in 1930, with a story
all its own, laid in Russia, with Lawrence Tibbett and
Grace Moore as the principals. In 1940 the same studio
remade it, going back to the original story as a vehicle for
Jeanette MacDonald and Nelson Eddy.

Sometime in 1928, Laurence Stallings, who with Max-
well Anderson had written the unforgettable *What Price
Glory*, suggested to Hammerstein that they write a musical
show together. He knew how to write a play, but he needed
Oscar II to turn it into a vehicle suitable for music—and,
of course, to write lyrics. He even had a story, laid in the
days of the '49 gold rush. "And I've got a very unusual
leading man. You see, this fellow's a killer." Completely
captivated by this notion, Hammerstein accepted on the
spot. Vincent Youmans agreed to write the music, and the
trio forthwith went to work on the new show, which they
called *Rainbow*.

By the end of September, 1928, Oscar II had three productions running in New York: *Show Boat*, at the Ziegfeld; *Good Boy*, at Hammerstein's; and *New Moon*, at the
Imperial. Then came the night of the first of November,

and the law of averages tapped him gently on the shoulder. The occasion was Philip Goodman's production of *Rainbow*, at the Gallo Theatre. The cast was good, including Harland Dixon, Charles Ruggles, Brian Donlevy, and Libby Holman. Youmans' score was one of his best. The critics sensed the merits of the book—thus Barnes, in the *Herald Tribune*: "A prodigal, bright-hued entertainment . . . with absorbing melodramatic overtones which burst through the thin veil of a graceful score and pretty dances" —and Gabriel, in the *American*: "Too hearty for quibbling, too big to be trifled with"—and Littell, in the *Post*: "The best of 'Rainbow' is wonderfully good and also brand new, and for that Laurence Stallings, who wrote its book, must be credited with one of the most refreshingly original musical comedies on record."

With all that in its favor, *Rainbow* lasted for exactly twenty-nine performances, Hammerstein's worst failure since *New Toys*.

The truth is, I think, that *Rainbow* was ahead of its time. The very qualities that the critics praised—originality, melodramatic overtones, realistic speech and action— were those that the theatergoing public was not yet ready to enjoy. The people of *Show Boat* had been real enough, but they spoke the language of romance. *Rainbow* was rougher, tougher stuff, the direct ancestor of *South Pacific*. But whereas Bloody Mary's reference to "steengy bastards" arouses hilarity today, the major's line at the end of *Rainbow*'s first act—"The son of a bitch shot me"—left the audience of its day shocked and disapproving.

Early in 1927, some time before Jerome Kern's memorable *Show Boat* telephone call, Oscar Hammerstein was preparing to leave for London, to oversee the Drury Lane production of *Desert Song*. His stateroom on the *Berengaria* engaged, and his bags practically packed, he devoted a part of his farewell week at his Great Neck, Long Island, home to a neighborly game of touch football. Hammerstein's team stuck to the American football rules, whereas the opposing team, headed by Leslie Howard and Philip Merivale, insisted on playing the English soccer rules. Under the circumstances, it was hardly surprising that Hammerstein managed to sprain his ankle so badly that he was obliged to cancel his *Berengaria* reservation and take the next boat. He still regards touch football as one of the finest of outdoor sports; for on that "next" boat he met Australian-born Dorothy Blanchard, who had appeared in the first *Charlot Revue* and was currently a successful interior decorator. As he sums it up: no touch football, no sprained ankle; no sprained ankle, no cancellation; no cancellation, no next boat; no next boat, no Dorothy Blanchard. Both obtained divorces in 1928, and on March 14, 1929, they were married. Like the Richard Rodgers', they still are.

Another event—perhaps not so far-reaching but memorable—took place in 1929. This was Arthur Hammerstein's production of *Sweet Adeline*, billed as "A musical romance of the Gay Nineties, book and lyrics by Oscar Hammerstein II, with music by Jerome Kern." It was the peaceful tale of a girl who sings at her father's beer garden, falls in love with a sailor who goes off to the Spanish-American War, goes into musical comedy, makes a hit, and finds her true love in the backer of the show. Helen Morgan was the

girl, Irene Franklin was a slangy actress, and Charles Butterworth was the principal comedian. The author had arranged three comedy exits for Butterworth of which he was
very proud, and which never failed to bring down the
house.

On the evening of October 29, 1929, *Sweet Adeline*
had been running at Hammerstein's Theatre for eight
weeks. The notices had been ecstatic, and the piece was
selling out nightly, with a heavy advance sale. Then an
extraordinary thing happened. Butterworth made his three
exits to dead silence. Wall Street had crashed that afternoon, and nobody was laughing. Thanks to the advance
sale, *Sweet Adeline* managed to run until March, 1930.
It had no successor for three years.

Those three paradoxical years saw the Great Depression
and the Great Gold Rush running side by side. The success
of Al Jolson in *The Jazz Singer*, in 1927, had set off a
chain reaction among the studios. Sound pictures were
obviously here to stay, and their advent created a tremen-
dous demand for everybody and everything connected with
auditory entertainment. A horde of dramatic and vocal
coaches, composers, lyric writers, and publishers began a
great trek to the Golconda of the West Coast.

Hammerstein and Romberg were in an excellent strategic position, inasmuch as one of their musicals, *Desert
Song,* had already been made into a sensationally successful picture. If they could do it once, they could do it again.
So reasoned Warner Brothers, who forthwith obtained their
signatures to a breath-taking contract. They were to make
four pictures within two years, they were to have the final

say as to cutting, and their word was law concerning screen plays, lyrics, and music. In return, each was to receive one hundred thousand dollars a picture, against royalties.

Their first offering was *Viennese Nights*, a technicolor affair released in 1930, featuring Vivienne Segal and Walter Pidgeon. Hammerstein had written the book as well as the lyrics, and Romberg had turned out three songs as well as a vast quantity of incidental music, including a symphony that lasted seven minutes. That chore accomplished, Hammerstein returned to New York to join Morrie Ryskind in directing *The Gang's All Here*, a musical comedy with a book by Russel Crouse, lyrics by Owen Murphy and Robert Simon, and music by Lewis Gensler.

He stayed in New York long enough to see *The Gang* open and close in three weeks; then back to Hollywood, in 1931, to work with Romberg on another Vitaphone picture, *Children of Dreams*.

By this time the gold rush was over. The studios had rather overdone the making of musical pictures, and the customers were in a state of open revolt. The situation had arrived at the point where the movie houses were commencing to hang out signs, "No music in this picture," as a bait for the public.

It was then that Warner Brothers approached the two, and, according to Hammerstein, said, in effect: "Do you boys really *insist* on making two more pictures?" They finally reached a compromise whereby each received one hundred thousand dollars to cancel the contract—as Hammerstein rather wistfully remarks, "The most money I ever got for *not* making two pictures."

Back in New York, he promptly invested most of his loot in two musical comedies. The first, *Free for All,* had Laurence Schwab as collaborator on the book, with a score by Richard Whiting. Schwab and Mandel presented it at the Manhattan Theatre on September 8, 1931. It lasted for fifteen performances. The second, presented by the same producers at the same theater on October 27 of that year, was *East Wind,* book and lyrics by Oscar II and Frank Mandel, music by Romberg. It closed after twenty-three performances. This, in a way, was a record, inasmuch as in the space of five weeks he had managed to achieve a loss of eighty thousand dollars with two failures. There was some consolation in a six-months' run of *Show Boat,* which Ziegfeld revived the following spring. But the sting of defeat still smarted.

The sting was definitely drawn on the evening of November 8, 1932, when Peggy Fears presented *Music in the Air* at the Alvin Theatre. Besides providing the book, lyrics, and music, Hammerstein and Jerome Kern had directed the production. The story was simple but effective: Karl Reder (Walter Slezak), the schoolmaster of a small Bavarian town, is in love with Sieglinde (Katherine Carrington), the daughter of Doctor Lessing (Al Shean), a music teacher and composer. Karl writes the words for Doctor Lessing's latest song, and he and Sieglinde walk to Munich to find a publisher for it. There they meet Frieda (Natalie Hall), a musical comedy star, and her lover, Bruno Mahler (Tullio Carminati), a playwright. He tries to make Sieglinde the star of his new operetta, while Frieda develops a none-too-sisterly interest in Karl. Sieglinde is engaged for the role, and her father comes to town to be in at the rehearsals. He gets under everybody's feet and makes a general nuisance of himself, while it is obvious that Sieglinde will never be a professional. Eventually she and her father and Karl return happily home, to their (and everyone else's) relief.

This slight plot is worth retelling in that it points a moral; not a heavily stressed one, to be sure, but present just the same—as it is present in most of Hammerstein's recent librettos. In this case it served to convey his detestation of amateurs and dilettantes. He reverted to this topic in two subsequent shows—with dubious success.

The critics were unanimous in their approval of *Music in the Air*. Oscar II points out that he got good notices for the book of a show for the first time in years—Brooks Atkinson in the *Times*, for instance:

At last the musical drama has been emancipated. . . . Without falling back into the cliches of the trade, he has written sentiment and comedy that are tender and touching. It is an amusing story and an effortless piece of craftsmanship, and it provides a perfect setting for Mr. Kern's score.

The Kern music also had its particular accolade. At least four of the numbers—"I've Told Ev'ry Little Star," "And Love Was Born," "Egern on the Tegern See," and "The Song Is You"—are still making the rounds after twenty-one years.

The piece ran eighteen weeks at the Alvin Theatre, closed briefly, and ran twenty-four weeks at the Forty-fourth Street Theatre, where it closed on September 16,

1933, after a New York run of eleven months. A West Coast company played Los Angeles and San Francisco, and C. B. Cochran produced it in London in the spring of 1933. Fox Films made a picture of it in 1934, with Gloria Swanson and Douglass Montgomery in the leading roles.

*Music in the Air* was followed by a long, lean period —ten years during which he wrote six musical comedies, and adapted or produced three others, without registering a single solid hit. In the spring of 1933 he had gone to England to stage the London production of *Music in the Air*. The production safely launched, he paid a flying visit (not literally) to Berlin, where he saw an operetta called *Ball at the Savoy*. The book (which bore a striking family resemblance to *Die Fledermaus*) was by Alfred Gruenwald and Fritz Loehner-Beda, with music by Paul Abraham. He took a fancy to the show, and wrote an English version with English lyrics which was produced at the Drury Lane Theatre.

The London *Times* critic remarked:

The scenery . . . was very good. The music . . . was very good. The plot was very good. The dialogue, which never stopped except when somebody sang, was very good, and very good, too, was the acting and everything else connected with this show. A jaundiced view would be that the scenery was . . . pre-anybody with any kind of taste. That the music was . . . exactly what we have been hearing for years. . . . That the plot bored to tears even our grandmothers. That the dialogue had not a line of wit from beginning to end.

The other critics were similarly calm. Which may help to explain why, despite the efforts of Maurice Evans and

Natalie Hall, who played the leading roles, the piece lasted an insufficient sixteen weeks.

Returning briefly to the States, he was invited by Otto Harbach to collaborate on the book of what turned out to be *Roberta*. Instead, he worked with Jerome Kern on *Three Sisters*, a musical comedy that was produced at Drury Lane on April 9, 1934. The comments of the critics were again of the "uh-huh" variety, and the sororal trio departed after a stay of two months.

Sadder and wiser—and poorer—after having written two *succès d'estime,* he returned to Hollywood and the welcoming arms of M-G-M for refueling. His first assignment was *The Night Is Young,* a picture released early in 1935, for which he and Sigmund supplied lyrics and music. The script, adapted from a story by Vicki Baum, was variation number 1,001 of the gent-with-royal-blood-falls-in-love-with-commoner-marries-another-for-reasons-of-state plot. It did have its piquant moments and original twists—until the Hayes Office went to work on it. It is survived by a famous Hammerstein-Romberg song, "When I Grow Too Old to Dream."

Meanwhile he worked with Romberg on the score of *May Wine,* which Laurence Schwab produced at the St. James Theatre, New York, on December 5, 1935 The book, by Frank Mandel, was based on a story by Wallace Smith and Eric Von Stroheim. Richard Lockridge's review in the New York *Sun* sums up what the critics thought of it:

The whole thing manages to be, at one and the same time, slightly clotted with plot and rather vapory. There is so much story, and all of it is so obviously absurd, and the elimination of the dancing girls leaves so much time to be filled in that I could never quite keep my mind on it.

It did, however, have a mildly successful run of six months.

On his return to Hollywood Oscar II found that M-G-M had nothing with which to occupy him at the moment, but that Paramount did. M-G-M finally released him, on condition that Paramount paid him more than M-G-M had—a purely friendly gesture that was unheard-of among the studios.

In 1936-37 he worked on three pictures for Paramount —not counting a screen version of *The Count of Luxembourg* that was never filmed. The first of the three was *Give Us This Night,* for which he supplied lyrics for music by Erich Wolfgang Korngold. Gladys Swarthout played the role of a beautiful opera singer (which should not have been too difficult), with Jan Kiepura as a young fisherman whose voice she discovers. In view of Mr. Kiepura's violet-like modesty, it is to be hoped that no one showed him Kate Cameron's observation in the New York *Daily News*: "A little too much of Jan Kiepura . . . hardly enough of Gladys Swarthout."

Number two was *Swing High, Swing Low,* for which Hammerstein collaborated with Virginia Van Upp on a script based on the famous stage play, *Burlesque.* No less than six song writers combined to supply the lyrics and music.

Number three was *High, Wide, and Handsome,* a tale of the Pennsylvania oil fields for which he wrote both the script and the lyrics, with music by Kern. He was a little dubious about the assignment, remarking that "oil and music don't mix." Nor did they. The combination of a highly melodramatic story with Kern's smoothly lyric melodies was not a wholly successful one.

In '38 Hammerstein returned East to work with Harbach and Kern on *Gentleman Unafraid,* a pageant-like musical play that had been commissioned by the St. Louis Municipal Theater Association. It was a Civil War story concerning the heart-searchings of a group of Southern West Point cadets, torn between their loyalty to their native South and their duty to the North, which has trained them. One of them joins the Union side, and later captures a spy who is the brother of the girl he loves. The synopsis concludes with the slightly startling announcement that "with the end of the war, and the assassination of Lincoln, all is righted."

The piece was presented at the Municipal Opera in St. Louis on June 3, 1938, and ran one week—which was all it was supposed to run. Harbach, however, refused to let the matter drop, and made vain attempts to have it produced elsewhere, writing several new versions in the course of his efforts. It never had another professional production, but it is still performed occasionally by college dramatic groups.

After heeding a hurry call from M-G-M to write the lyrics for *The Great Waltz,* a picture based on the life story of Johann Strauss the Younger, he joined forces with Laurence Schwab in producing *Glorious Morning,* a play based on the Joan of Arc story, and *Knights of Song,* a dramatization of the careers of Gilbert and Sullivan. Since nothing much came of these efforts, he beat a strategic retreat to Hollywood, where he rounded out 1938 by doing some work on *The Story of Vernon and Irene Castle*, which R.K.O. released as a starring vehicle for Fred Astaire and Ginger Rogers. Incidentally, the thought of that picture has always aroused poignant memories in the breast of the author of this book, to whom Miss Rogers loaned the script, with the request for a Frank Opinion. The frank opinion was to the effect that Miss Rogers would be out of her mind to make the film, since it was bound to be a dismal failure. The reader may possibly not need to be reminded that it was a resounding success.

The release of the Rogers-Astaire picture, in the spring of 1939, found Hammerstein and Kern hard at work on a new musical, which they called *Very Warm for May*. Max Gordon produced it at the Alvin Theatre on November 17, with a cast headed by Donald Brian and including Hiram Sherman and Eve Arden. Hammerstein had directed the book as well as writing it. The story concerned a summer stock company in New England that was nearly wrecked by the inept direction of an arty impresario—Hammerstein again baring his teeth at dilettantes.

The critical verdict was five to three, ranging from: "Never, I think, have elements so promising been tangled more hopelessly in the barbed wire of a thoroughly exasperating plot" (Lockridge, *Sun*), to: "Its behavior is civilized, its humor sanitary, and its manners good. . . . The plot keeps the stage going without getting in everybody's way . . . pretty glowing" (Anderson, New York *American*). The public supported the negative verdict, and *Very Warm for May* departed after seven weeks, leaving behind only the memorable song, "All the Things You Are."

The New York World's Fair, in Flushing Meadows, ended its first season on October 31, 1939. While it had been far from a profitable investment, moneywise, nevertheless public interest had been so steadily on the increase that the World's Fair Corporation decided to gamble on a second season. Furthermore, to make certain that Billy Rose's Aquacade would not be the only cultural exhibit, it was decided to present something in the nature of a pageant of American history.

The fair reopened on May 11, 1940. The pageant, entitled *American Jubilee*, opened the following evening, the list of those involved in its creation reading like a page from the theatrical *Who's Who*. The book and lyrics were by Oscar Hammerstein II, with music by Arthur Schwartz; Albert Johnson was designer and producer; the costumes were by Lucinda Ballard; Leonidoff was stage director; and Don Voorhees conducted the orchestra. The *Jubilee* presented a series of American historical highlights, centering about such famous events and people as George Washington and his inauguration, P. T. Barnum and Jenny Lind, Diamond Jim Brady and Lillian Russell, Abraham Lincoln, Joe Jackson, the hobo cyclist, Teddy Roosevelt and his Rough Riders, and James Melton's collection of ancient automobiles. The finale presented Ray Middleton's inauguration as President in 1941.

Despite an opening night that compelled the participants to perform in a driving rain, the pageant was a huge success, both with the critics and the customers, and paid its way until the closing of the fair, the following October.

It was that same year of 1940 that Hammerstein wrote

the only song of his that was not part of a musical comedy score: "The Last Time I Saw Paris." As a youngster he had accompanied his father, Willy Hammerstein, on one of his talent-scouting trips, and had stayed briefly in the French capital (at the Grand Hotel). "The next time I saw Paris," he says, "I was seventeen, touring Europe with some other young fellows. We promenaded and did the theaters. Once a tall, dark girl, alone at a sidewalk café table, smiled at me and said something. I didn't know the rules, didn't know what was expected of me. So I ran like hell." Later he regained his courage and lived for five months in an apartment near the Etoile. So he knew his Paris, as the touching verses that he wrote about her will testify. The music, it has always seemed to one listener, ranks far below the words. Kern was not used to setting music to words. In his work with Hammerstein the tune had always come first. Now, faced with the necessity of reversing the process, he followed the words, but didn't enhance them. It has been said that he was trying to imitate a Paris cabaret song. But Paris cabaret songs, however banal, are written with a sort of shabby sincerity. They have a mood. In setting "The Last Time I Saw Paris," Kern, it seems, captured the banality but missed the mood.

Came 1941, and a new Hammerstein-Romberg opus— the last of its kind, as later events proved. After a week's summer tryout in St. Louis and a three-day sojourn in New Haven, Connecticut, Max Gordon presented *Sunny River* at the St. James Theatre on December 4. The story: Marie, a New Orleans café singer in the 1860's, and Jean, a society leader, are in love. Cecille, who is after Jean, tells Marie that Jean and herself have been lovers. Marie then goes to Paris and becomes a famous singer. Then she returns to Jean, who enlists in Stonewall Jackson's army. At the close, the girls mourn him together.

The critics were in a vicious mood: "Dull and commonplace" (*Herald Tribune*) . . . "to say the evening depressed me would be to indulge in a form of understatement" (*Telegram*) . . . "one of the worst books with which musical comedy has been burdened in recent years" (*Daily News*) . . . "paying a duty call on entertainment" (*Times*). John Anderson, in the *Journal-American*, remarked, briefly, "Sunny River, stay 'way from my door." After four weeks and four days *Sunny River* disappeared.

This was a period of something approaching despair for Hammerstein. Nine lean years had passed since his last hit, *Music in the Air*. They were not lean years, financially—the movies had taken care of that. But they were years of frustration, of a vain attempt to capture the wholehearted attention of his audience. Had he an audience? Had the parade passed him by? It was in this gloomy mood that he retreated to his Sabine farm in Bucks County, Pennsylvania, to think things over.

At that time, it so happened, Dorothy Hammerstein's services as interior decorator were in such demand as to keep her in New York during most of her week days, leaving Oscar II with a good deal of unoccupied time on his hands. Some obscure impulse prompted him to buy a complete recording of *Carmen*. Or perhaps it was not so obscure. *Carmen*, which had always been his favorite opera, is not so far removed, in form, from *Show Boat* or *New Moon*

*143*

as you might think. Its music is heavier in texture, the dialogue briefer and more pointed—but it *could* be called an operetta with a tragic ending. And it is not to be wondered at that Hammerstein, for consolation, should play it over and over again—which he did, until he knew the whole work practically by heart.

It suddenly occurred to him to try his hand at a new *Carmen*, in which the story would remain unchanged while the actors and the setting would become American. He called it *Carmen Jones*, and worked on it for several months. It was practically a labor of love. For the first time in his career he was writing a stage piece that had not been commissioned. Who the producer might be he did not know, or care. He even thought of producing it himself, on a very small scale.

And then, one day in the summer of 1942, he had a telephone call. . . .

# Part Three

It was the early summer of 1942, and the Theatre Guild was unhappy. A succession of wrong guesses during the preceding season had resulted in a succession of theatrical failures that had brought New York's famous producing organization dangerously close to insolvency. The Guild's next production *must* be a hit. In this crisis its directors, Lawrence Langner and Theresa Helburn, bethought themselves of Lynn Riggs's play *Green Grow the Lilacs*. As produced by them previously, it had been agreeable but somewhat lacking in substance. However, it seemed to have possibilities as the book for a musical comedy. Granted that, who would write the lyrics and music? Who would come the nearest to being the guarantee of a successful job?

Those were, of course, rhetorical questions. The obvious choice was the fabulously successful team of Rodgers and Hart, whose latest offering (incidentally, the biggest hit of their joint career), *By Jupiter*, had just got off to a roaring start at the Shubert Theatre. Rodgers had liked the Lynn Riggs play, and enthusiastically accepted the invitation to provide the music for its new version. His partner, however, was another story.

Lorenz Hart was a lonely, frustrated man, who had never quite become adjusted to life—a man who gave fabulous parties at which he seemed to play the role of an uninvited guest. He was sensitive about his height (he was barely five feet tall), and like so many undersized men tried to conceal it—in his case, by wearing lifts in his shoes and smoking specially made, extra-long cigars. On the other hand, he exhibited none of the loud talk and bluster that are the usual symptoms of overcompensation. Rodgers describes him as "a brilliant conversationalist, full of wit and charm, and one of the kindest and most tolerant men I have ever known."

Over the years his health had steadily deteriorated, and his overstrung nerves made him erratic and unpredictable. An appointment with him was a gamble. Even when the two were at work on a new show, he might suddenly disappear for days at a time. Rodgers' attitude toward him was a mixture of elder brother (he was seven years Hart's junior) and governess, deferring to his talent and indulgent toward his eccentricities. There were times when he would compose an entire score before being able to induce Hart to provide the lyrics. Hart was hospitalized during the writing of *By Jupiter*; and in order to finish the job on time, Rodgers took a guest room at Doctors Hospital, and had a piano moved in, so that they could go to work.

Hart's answer to the Guild's suggestion was a dismayed negative. He pleaded that he had just finished putting on one show, was just out of the hospital, and was worn out. He wanted to go to Mexico for a rest. If Dick really wanted to do the new show, by all means let him do it. But please, for this once, get another lyrist—and no hard feelings. Rodgers reluctantly agreed, and Hart went off to Mexico.

There is a legend to the effect that the Theatre Guild

On September 23, 1924, Arthur Hammerstein presented *Rose Marie* at the Imperial Theatre. It closed in 1926, after 557 performances. Oscar II shared the book and lyrics with Otto Harbach, the music was by Rudolf Friml and Herbert Stothart. *Rose Marie* has become an internationally-known favorite. Mary Ellis, right, and Dennis King played the leads in the original production, singing the famous "Indian Love Call" together. The picture below shows the chorus line of "Totem Tom Tom," a popular number that involved girls dressed as totem poles. (Culver Service.)

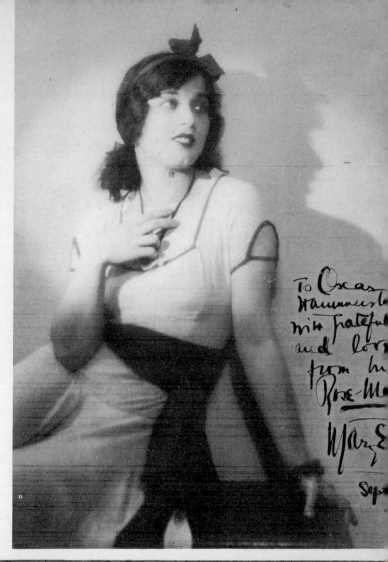

To Oscar
Hammerst[...]
with grateful
and lov[...]
from h[...]
Rose-M[...]

Mary E[...]

Sep[...]

In 1925, Oscar II with Jerome Kern had written another great hit, *Sunny*, produced by Charles Dillingham. *Sunny* ran for over a year and left behind the still popular song "Who." The picture shows the four principals: left to right, Jack Donahue, Marilyn Miller, Mary May and Clifton Webb. (Culver Service.)

Dennis King and Mary Ellis in the first production of *Rose Marie*. Their roles were played by Jeanette MacDonald and Nelson Eddy in the movie version made in 1936. (Culver Service.)

On the left are two comedians from *Wild Rose*, Gus Shy and Inez Courtney. (Culver Service.) The show, produced by Arthur Hammerstein, book and lyrics by Oscar II and Otto Harbach, music by Rudolf Friml, only lasted eight weeks. *Desert Song*, which opened in New York on November 30, 1926, twenty-nine days after *Wild Rose*, gave the Hammerstein-Harbach team the hit for that year; its run lasted for over a year. Below, Eddie Buzzell as society correspondent for the Paris *Tribune* looks unhappy on a donkey with Nellie Breen, who played his ward. (Culver Service.)

At right, a romantic moment from *Desert Song* shows William O'Neal with Margaret Irving and Lyle Evans. (Culver Service.)

Oscar Hammerstein II with composer Sigmund Romberg. (Albert Davis Collection.) Jerome Kern and Oscar Hammerstein; they wrote *Show Boat, Sunny, Sweet Adeline, Music in the Air,* and *Very Warm for May.* (Courtesy of Oscar Hammerstein II.)

*Show Boat* opened on December 27, 1927 and closed after 572 performances. With music by Jerome Kern, books and lyrics by Hammerstein, it was adapted from a novel by Edna Ferber. Picture shows Charles Winninger as Cap'n Andy. (Culver Service.)

Jules Bledsoe, in the role of Joe in *Show Boat*, sang "Ol' Man River." (Culver Service.)

Helen Morgan who played Julie in *Show Boat* and sang "Bill." (Culver Service.)

*New Moon,* a romantic musical comedy with music by Sigmund Romberg, opened in New York in November, 1929, and ran for 509 performances. Here is Evelyn Herbert in a suitably romantic gown. In this show she sang the all-time favorite "Lover, Come Back to Me." (Culver Service.)

Oscar Hammerstein II with his wife Dorothy. The picture below shows that Oscar likes to compose his lyrics standing up at his desk.

Billed as "musical adventure," *Music in the Air* opened in 1932 and ran for 342 performances. Book and lyrics by Hammerstein, music by Kern, they also staged the production. As the picture shows clearly, the setting was Bavarian. The cast included Walter Slezak, who sang "I've Told Every Little Star." (Courtesy of Oscar Hammerstein II.)

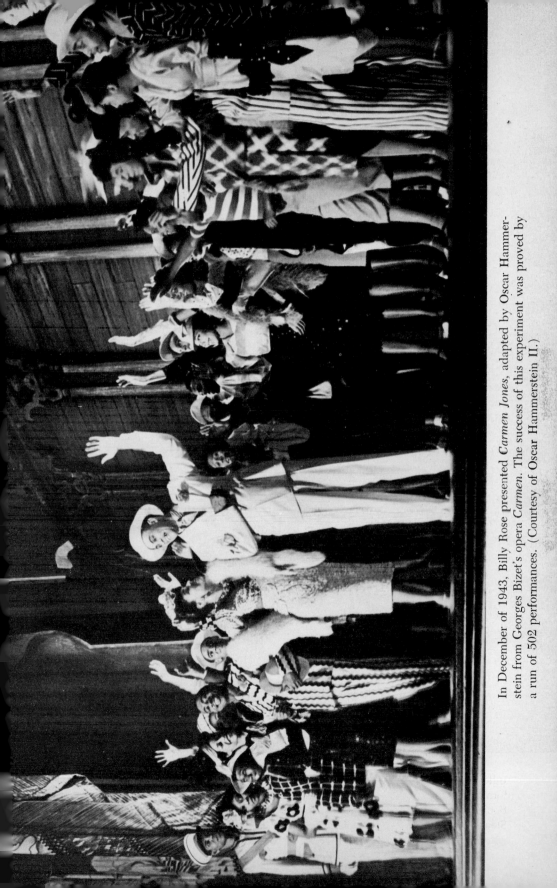

In December of 1943, Billy Rose presented *Carmen Jones*, adapted by Oscar Hammerstein from Georges Bizet's opera *Carmen*. The success of this experiment was proved by a run of 502 performances. (Courtesy of Oscar Hammerstein II.)

Richard Rodgers and Oscar Hammerstein II. Their collaboration started with the Theatre Guild production of *Oklahoma!* in 1943.

Oscar Hammerstein with Rouben Mamoulian, who directed *Oklahoma!* Below, Richard
Rodgers with Theresa Helburn and Lawrence Langner of the Theatre Guild. (Courtesy
of The Theatre Guild.) *Oklahoma!* was the Guild's first musical and one of its greatest
successes.

Celeste Holm, cast as Ado Annie Carnes, sang "I Cain't Say No."

brought Rodgers and Hammerstein together. This is not true. While they were not intimates, they had known each other for years, admired each other's work, and had even talked about working together sometime. In fact, they had been collaborators, back in 1920, when a song of theirs, "There's Always Room for One More," was inserted in the score of the Columbia varsity show of that year. It was a modest offering—even the authors are a bit uncertain as to how it went—but it was a beginning.

So it was no stranger to whom Rodgers telephoned a few days after Hart had departed to Mexico. Would Oscar have lunch with him? There was something he wanted to talk over.

Arrived at the Barberry Room, Rodgers came at once to the point: "The Guild is talking about making a musical show out of *Green Grow the Lilacs*. Larry and I are supposed to do the lyrics and music, but Larry wants no part of it. In fact, he's gone to Mexico. Will you read the play? I thought we might get together on it."

Hammerstein's reply was indicative of how closely their minds work together in matters theatrical. For he had already read *Green Grow the Lilacs* and was equally enthusiastic over its musical comedy possibilities. On his last visit to the West Coast he had, in fact, read the play aloud to Jerome Kern, sitting beside Kern's swimming pool. Jerry had listened politely, remarked that it had no third act—and that was that. Perhaps the late Jerome Kern and the late Larry Hart should get part of the credit for bringing Rodgers and Hammerstein together.

They set to work early in August of 1942, and hit it off

from the start. Rodgers has said, in an interview, "The important thing is what we gave each other creatively. The very first lyric that Oscar finished was 'Oh, What a Beautiful Mornin',' and when he handed it to me and I read it for the first time I was a little sick with joy because it was so lovely and so right. When you're given lines like 'The corn is as high as an elephant's eye,' you get something to say musically."

They labored under one serious handicap in writing the new piece: auditions. The audition is an occupational disease, or necessary evil, or whatever else you want to call it (watching your language, of course), that is traceable to the increasingly fantastic cost of producing shows, particularly musical shows. In the old days a producer who needed backing could usually get it by making half a dozen telephone calls. He still can, provided he has a reputation as a shrewd picker of hits. But at that moment the Guild had no such reputation. Its losing streak had made it a poor risk in the eyes of its usual backers. "Sight-unseen" money was painfully scarce. Furthermore, the average potential backer, accustomed to associating musical comedies with important stars, was frightened off by learning that this new production contemplated no stars.

It became dismally obvious that the Guild must resort to giving auditions. Rodgers and Hammerstein and the Guild directors would appear before an invited audience of prospective investors. Rodgers and his rehearsal pianist, Margot Hopkins, would play portions of the score on two pianos, while Hammerstein would narrate the story, and Alfred Drake and Joan Roberts would sing some of the songs. This went on for weeks, with discouragingly slow results. For one audition, before a particularly affluent group, the Guild hired a studio in Steinway Hall, and after the performance served caviar and champagne. The sole result was that one patron, who had subscribed a thousand dollars, did *not* ask for his money back. The rest expressed polite thanks and left without pledging a penny. (All this took up so much of the authors' time that six or seven of the songs had to be written during rehearsals.)

At last, after countless auditions, the money was raised, somehow, the cast was assembled and rehearsed, scenery and costumes were finished (the scene designer and the costumer gambling on a percentage of possible profits in lieu of cash), and the new piece, under the title of *Away We Go*, departed for its tryout of three nights in New Haven and two weeks in Boston. The final title, by the way, was agreed upon after the New Haven opening, the authors desiring to call the piece *Oklahoma* with the Guild consenting, provided an exclamation point be added. Meanwhile, however, all the "paper" for the tryout performances—posters, tickets, and programs—had already been printed; so that *Away We Go* did not become *Oklahoma!* until its New York debut.

In a way, an opening in New Haven is almost worse than a New York first night. In New York it is generally too late to do any tinkering with the show. Barring a few rare exceptions, it's a success or a failure. But a show trying out on the road is in a state of flux; and New Haven is only one and a half hours from New York. So up come a motley crew of observers—agents, backers, friends, hopers-for-the-worst—all self-appointed play doctors and all brimming with unsolicited advice. The opening of *Away We Go* was no exception. One well-wisher opined that all the show needed was some comedy. The costumer, coming out of the theater, remarked, "Nice little show you've got there—though of course it's not my kind of show." Kurt Weil just didn't like it. One prominent member of the company—never mind who—advised cutting out "People Will Say We're in Love," the ultimate big hit of the piece. One and all, they sat through about half the performance, then caught the late train back to New York, bearing the glad tidings that the show was not a success.

Boston was friendly and helpful—Rodgers has been quoted as saying, "I wouldn't open even a can of sardines except in Boston." There is a legend to the effect that *Oklahoma!* narrowly missed closing before coming into New York, the implication being that its audiences didn't like it. On the contrary, it had enthusiastic houses from the start. There is this much truth to the legend: When *Oklahoma!* opened in New Haven the money to meet its production cost had not yet been fully subscribed. The remaining necessary funds were raised during its stay in Boston. It's superfluous to point out that the Guild directors were under a terrific nervous strain.

For Rodgers and Hammerstein it was simply a matter of going through another tryout. They had faith in their work, and being veterans in the musical comedy field—fifty-nine productions between them—were prepared to correct any number of minor faults. That's what tryouts are for. But this was the Guild's first big musical—and a vitally important one. It was within the range of possibilities that the end of *Oklahoma!* might be the end of the Guild. Small wonder that its directors had a bad case of production jitters. Improvements were made that didn't improve. Scenes were cut and then restored. The success of *Oklahoma!* was desperately important to everyone; and everything that desperation could accomplish was tried out. The authors good-naturedly consented to rewrite scenes that didn't need rewriting, until, as Hammerstein remarks, "Even our wives deserted us. They would huddle in corners, whispering, 'They're ruining the show,' 'We ought to tell them,' 'Will you?' 'Shall I?' "

At last Rodgers took to walking the Guild directors up and down after the performance. "Now let's analyze the show. Take the first number, 'Oh, What a Beautiful Mornin'.' That goes all right, doesn't it? Take the next, 'The Surrey with the Fringe on Top.' Nothing wrong with that, is there? Or 'Kansas City.' They like that, don't they? Or the ballets. They stop the show, don't they? People laugh and applaud all through, don't they? We're selling out, aren't we? What more do you want?"

Still apprehensive, the Guild presented *Oklahoma!* at the St. James Theatre in New York, on Wednesday evening, March 31, 1943. Agnes De Mille, in her enchanting autobiography, *Dance to the Piper*, tells how it all began:

The first night was by no means sold out. The Guild subscription had fallen very low. I had ten front-row balcony seats and I didn't know whom to give them to. I think a couple remained empty. They stood alongside of me, Rodgers and the staff. Oscar, who was calm, sat with his wife. . . . The curtain went up on a woman churning butter; a very fine baritone came on stage singing the closest thing to lieder our theater has produced. He sang exquisitely with his whole heart about what a morning in our Southwest is like. At the end, people gave an audible sigh and looked at one another—this had seldom happened before. It was music. They sat right back and opened their hearts. The show rolled.

On the next page you will find the program of that—as it turned out—historic evening:

In view of *Oklahoma!*'s subsequent history, the notices take on an added interest; and be it said here that the critics came through with such notices as had not been seen in these parts since the day after *Show Boat* opened. In the *Times*, Lewis Nichols summed up the collective verdict rather neatly: "A truly delightful musical play . . . simple and warm. Possibly, in addition to being a musical play, 'Oklahoma!' could be called a folk opera. Whatever it is, it is very good."

To quote the others at any length would be repetitious. Let these excerpts suffice: "A jubilant and enchanting musical" (Barnes, *Herald Tribune*) . . . "fresh and imaginative, as enchanting to the eye as Richard Rodgers' music is to the ear" (Anderson, New York *American*) . . . "fresh, lively, colorful, and enormously pleasing" (Rascoe, *World-Telegram*) . . . "fresh and diverting . . . charming . . . tunely" (Morehouse, New York *Sun*) . . . "the most thoroughly and attractively American musical comedy since 'Show Boat' . . . really is different . . . beautifully different" (Mantle, *News*) . . . "a completely enchanting performance . . . gay, stylish, imaginative . . . my gratitude is practically boundless" (Gibbs, *New Yorker*).

170

# ST. JAMES THEATRE

138 West 48th Street Theatre Co. Inc.

THE · PLAYBILL · A · WEEKLY · PUBLICATION · OF · PLAYBILL · INCORPORATED

Week beginning Sunday, November 7, 1943    •    Matinees Thursday and Saturday

## THE THEATRE GUILD

presents

# OKLAHOMA!

A Musical Play

Based on the play "Green Grow the Lilacs" by Lynn Riggs

Music by RICHARD RODGERS
Book and Lyrics by OSCAR HAMMERSTEIN 2d
Production directed by ROUBEN MAMOULIAN
Dances by AGNES de MILLE

Settings by
LEMUEL AYERS

Costumes by
MILES WHITE

Production supervised by
LAWRENCE LANGER and THERESA HELBURN

With

| | | | |
|---|---|---|---|
| BETTY GARDE | ALFRED DRAKE | JOSEPH BULOFF | JOAN ROBERTS |
| LEE DIXON | HOWARD da SILVA | CELESTE HOLM | RALPH RIGGS |
| | MARC PLATT | KATHARINE SERGAVA | |

Orchestra directed by J. S. Blackton
Orchestrations by Russell Bennett

## CAST
(In Order of Appearance)

| | | | |
|---|---|---|---|
| AUNT ELLER | BETTY GARDE | ELLEN | KATHARINE SERGAVA |
| CURLY | ALFRED DRAKE | KATE | ELLEN LOVE |
| LAUREY | JOAN ROBERTS | SYLVIE | JOAN McCRACKEN |
| IKE SKIDMORE | BARRY KELLEY | ARMINA | KATE FRIEDLICH |
| FRED | EDWIN CLAY | AGGIE | BAMBI LINN |
| SLIM | HERBERT RISSMAN | ANDREW CARNES | RALPH RIGGS |
| WILL PARKER | LEE DIXON | CORD ELAM | OWEN MARTIN |
| JUD FRY | HOWARD da SILVA | JESS | VLADIMIR KOSTENKO |
| ADO ANNIE CARNES | CELESTE HOLM | CHALMERS | MARC PLATT |
| ALI HAKIM | JOSEPH BULOFF | MIKE | PAUL SHIERS |
| GERTIE CUMMINGS | VIRGINIA BOLEN | JOE | HAROLD GORDON |
| | SAM | ARTHUR ULISSE | |

The only minority report was brought in by Miss Wilella Waldorf, of the New York *Post*. It wasn't precisely damning, but the praise was pretty faint: "After a mild, somewhat monotonous beginning, 'Oklahoma!' suddenly comes to life about the middle of the first act. . . . Rodgers' songs are pleasant enough, but still manage to sound quite a bit alike . . . without much variety in the presentation."

Just what is *Oklahoma!*? Lewis Nichols calls it a folk opera. In its flavor and mood, possibly yes. Technically, no; for the word "opera" connotes something a good deal more pretentious than even its creators would claim it to be. Nor is it *opéra comique*; for in true *opéra comique*, such as *Carmen* and *Manon*, the percentage of spoken dialogue is very small. That nasty word "operetta" implies an element of artificiality of which *Oklahoma!* is innocent. It is musical comedy in the sense that occasionally the story is halted by a scene (the shotgun engagement of Ado Annie and Hakim, for instance) inserted for its own entertainment value. On the other hand, a character such as Jud Fry is far from being the conventional "menace" of musical comedy. Jud exists; he is flesh and blood; he is evil and pitiful. He serves to add realism to entertainment. So perhaps one might call *Oklahoma!* what its creators call it: a musical play. After all, they ought to know. Its archetypes are *Show Boat* and *Rainbow* and *Pal Joey* rather than *New Moon* and *On Your Toes*.

One factor that serves to integrate the action of *Oklahoma!* that makes it seem "all of a piece," so to speak, is the handling of the lyrics and music. The score of *Show Boat* contains twenty musical numbers, all different—a feast of lovely tunes that punctuate the action without necessarily advancing it. It is almost *too* tuneful. The score of *Oklahoma!* comprises just twelve basic musical numbers. But these twelve are not just—to use a fancy English adoption of a French word that doesn't exist—reprised. They are woven in and out of the story, sometimes under dialogue, sometimes quoted briefly, at others repeated in various guises (the Dream Ballet is built out of six of those numbers). All in all, this treatment of words and music allows them to function almost as leading motives, giving the story extraordinary unity and plausibility.

Is all this too solemn an approach to a wisp of lighthearted entertainment? Possibly. On the other hand, any theatrical work that can sweep the world as this one has done must possess values that deserve to be taken seriously. *Oklahoma!* closed at the St. James Theatre on May 29, 1948, after a New York run of 2,202 performances—five years and nine weeks—the longest continuous run of any musical entertainment in the history of the theater. Much had happened during those five years. Franklin D. Roosevelt and George Patton were dead. So were Henry Ford and Al Capone. World War II had been over for nearly three years. The eleven Nazi leaders had been tried and sentenced for their war crimes. The State of Israel had been proclaimed. On May 31, 1948, two days after the close of the New York run, the company took to the road, closing in Boston in May of 1949—a year's run. In April, 1947, a London company opened at Drury Lane, where it ran for 1,511 performances —three and a half years. It is still touring the provinces. A South African company played the season of 1948-49, while

173

an Australian company ran from 1948 to 1951. *Oklahoma!* has played in Norway, Sweden, and Denmark, and has been produced for the armed forces in Germany. A so-called National Company was assembled and started on the road in the fall of 1943. It closed for a summer layoff in the spring of 1952, after eight years and six months, to reopen in the early fall of that year. On March 31, 1953 it rounded out its tenth year, having been seen by more than eight million people and grossed over $15,000,000—and still going strong.

Just what is the ultimate secret of this musical play that can appeal to audiences in every part of the world (Italy, France, and Spain will doubtless capitulate sooner or later)? Here is a possible hint, from Lionel Hale's review, in the *Daily Mail*, of the London production:

This smash hit is not an evening of stars. It is color plus music plus wit plus dancing, put together with a sort of inspired single-mindedness to re-create on stage the young people of a youthful part of the earth.

It is youth that *Oklahoma!* brings to us; youth, and something else that this puzzled and bedeviled world is so desperately looking for—hope.

Even though Rodgers and Hart had failed to see eye to eye regarding *Oklahoma!* there was no thought of any permanent breach between them. Rodgers in particular was anxious to make some gesture to signify that the old partnership was still in existence. Accordingly, as soon as his partner had returned from the Mexican trip he proposed that they revive *A Connecticut Yankee*. Hart, pleased (and probably reassured), went to work at once. Together, they wrote six new songs for the forthcoming production, including "To Keep My Love Alive," which Vivienne Segal was to make famous. Rodgers himself was the producer, presenting the *Yankee* at the Martin Beck Theatre on the evening of November 17, 1943.

It was to prove a tragic opening night. Hart refused a seat, saying that he would rather stand at the back of the house. About halfway through the first act he turned and quietly left the theater. That was Wednesday night. No one knows what he did or where he went during the ensuing forty-eight hours, until he was found on Friday night, unconscious in his hotel room. He was rushed to the hospital, where he was treated with the (then) scarce and costly drug, penicillin. But it was too late. He died of double pneumonia on Monday, November 22, in his forty-ninth year. The old partnership was dissolved.

When Hammerstein had finished *Carmen Jones*, early in 1942, he had toyed with the idea of producing it himself, on a very modest scale. However, in the course of his ponderings he showed the script to Billy Rose. Mr. Rose, who has never been accused of failing to recognize a good thing when he sees it, promptly snatched it up.

The story, for the benefit of those who may not have seen *Carmen Jones*, is an extraordinarily adroit adaptation of the Meilhac-Halévy libretto. The cigarette factory in Seville becomes a parachute factory in a Southern town during World War II. Don José becomes Joe, a Negro corporal, while Escamillo emerges as Husky Miller, a heavyweight fighter. Carmen Jones, who works in the factory, steals Joe from Cindy Lou, the girl back home. The two run away to

Chicago, where Carmen transfers her fickle affection to Husky Miller. Joe begs her to return, but she abandons him. He kills her outside the arena on the night of Husky's championship fight. The recitatives are replaced with spoken dialogue, thus restoring the opera to its original form. One or two numbers are heard out of their usual order, but Bizet's score is played with no omissions or additions.

*Carmen Jones* opened its tryout run at the Erlanger Theatre in Philadelphia on October 19, 1943. It was enthusiastically received, the only somber note being struck by another famous producer who accosted Rose after the first performance and remarked: "You've got a great show there—but of course you'll have to have a new score."

"A new score? What do you mean?"

"Well, everybody knows *this* music."

Philadelphia, however, didn't seem to mind. The show spent three successful weeks at the Erlanger, then moved to Boston for three more, equally profitable.

*Carmen Jones* reached New York on December 2, 1943, where it opened at the Broadway Theatre. Hassard Short had supervised the staging, lighting, and color schemes of the production. The settings were by Howard Bay, the costumes by Raoul Pene du Bois; Eugene Loring had charge of the choreography, Robert Shaw had trained the chorus; and Joseph Lithau conducted.

The labors of this impressive-sounding staff had not been in vain. From some of the sterner music lovers there came yelps of pain over "this desecration of a classic"—but not nearly so many as might have been expected. The critics saw their duty and did it. The *Times*'s Lewis Nichols urged,

"Just call it wonderful, quite wonderful." Howard Barnes of the *Herald Tribune* averred that it "retains the score of the opera, but it clothes it with such miraculous showmanship that for once drama takes its rightful place in a music drama." Alton Cook of the *World-Telegram* called it "opera with the addition of a wild, primitive charm," and Robert Garland of the *Journal-American* described it as "a memorable milestone in the upward and onward course of the Great American showshop." According to Robert Coleman of the *Mirror*, it was "ever so much more wonderful and exciting than mere words can make it sound," and John Chapman of the *News* declared that it "rates all the adjectives that hurried fingers can find on a midnight keyboard. It is superb; it is enchantingly beautiful; it is musically exciting and visually stirring. Not once is 'Carmen Jones' wrong. Billy Rose, my hat is off to you and I bow low."

The public agreed. New York suddenly discovered a new musical team—Bizet and Hammerstein, and flocked to savor their product. People raved over *Carmen Jones* who had barely heard of *Carmen*. One of Producer Rose's Broadway cronies hailed him excitedly in the lobby of the theater: "Hey, Billy! D'ye know they're doing it at the Met in whiteface!"

*Carmen Jones* finally left the Broadway Theatre and headed for the road on December 27, 1945, after a New York run of a year and eleven weeks that had enriched everybody (except perhaps Bizet) who had had a hand in its creation.

Early in 1944 Rodgers and Hammerstein had opened an office in the R.K.O. Building at Fiftieth Street and the clumsily named Avenue of the Americas (which everyone still calls Sixth Avenue), where they planned to handle their correspondence and hold interviews and auditions. Then Dorothy Rodgers had an idea. So long as they had an office, why not, she suggested, become producers? The suggestion was probably not so shocking as it would have been to you or me, since both partners had already had some experience in the field. Rodgers had acted as coproducer, with Dwight Deere Wiman, of *By Jupiter*, and using the office of Chappell & Company, the music publishers, as headquarters, had produced the revival of *A Connecticut Yankee*. Arthur Hammerstein had produced no less than fourteen of his nephew's shows, so that Oscar II had had a chance to become thoroughly familiar with the details of play production. Accordingly, on October 19, 1944, the new firm made its bow at the Music Box Theatre with *I Remember Mama*, a play by John Van Druten based on Kathryn Forbes's book, *Mama's Bank Account*. It had a highly successful run and received three Donaldson Awards (similar to the Pulitzer Prizes and equally treasured): for the best direction of the season (Van Druten), the best settings (George Jenkins), and the best costumes (Lucinda Ballard).

The firm now occupies a ten-room suite of offices on Madison Avenue, and to date (early fall of 1953) has produced six plays and four musical comedies, of which eight had long runs. *Annie Get Your Gun*, produced in 1946, was hugely successful in New York, London, on the road, and as a picture. It collected Donaldson Awards for the best performance (Ethel Merman), best direction (Joshua Logan), and best score (Irving Berlin). Equally successful was *Happy Birthday*, starring Helen Hayes, which arrived in 1947. In *John Loves Mary*, also produced in 1947, Donaldson picked Tom Ewell as the best supporting actor. *The Happy Time*, which saw the light in 1949, got no awards, but it ran considerably over a year. Another 1949 production, *The Heart of the Matter*, fared worse, closing on the road without risking New York. John Steinbeck's *Burning Bright* (1950) came in, but was a little too heavily symbolical for its own good.

But to return to 1944. Rodgers and Hammerstein had opened their office, *I Remember Mama* was in the process of production, and *Oklahoma!* and *Carmen Jones* were off to a flying start. In other words, they were—for them—practically unemployed. They must, therefore, have welcomed the interruption when the Theatre Guild brought forth another play out of which, it was suggested, they might make a musical. This was Molnar's *Liliom*, which the Guild had first produced in 1921. The idea had a cool reception from Rodgers and Hammerstein at first, the consensus being that the story might be too tragic for a musical play. That problem solved (they solved it by adding a new final scene that was at least a satisfactory ending), came the question of where the scene of the play was to be laid. All four—Langner, Helburn, Rodgers, and Hammerstein—agreed that Budapest, where *Liliom* is originally laid, was too risky politically. Hungary might go Red, with disastrous repercussions upon a show laid in that country (and oh, how right they proved to be!).

Theresa Helburn, of the Guild, then suggested New

Orleans. But Hammerstein vetoed that. He couldn't see dealing with all those "zeez, zemz and zose." Finally, at one of their meetings, Rodgers announced, abruptly: "I've got it! New England."

And so to work. It was decided that the action would take place in a New England coastal town in the 1870's and '80's. This solved a problem for Hammerstein. As he has remarked, "In writing a musical show, one important thing is to find an excuse for the chorus." In the case of *Carousel* (its new name) this was easy. The girls were mill hands and the boys were fishermen.

One of the first musical numbers to be written was the famous soliloquy, near the close of the first act, in which Billy Bigelow makes plans for the future of his unborn child. As Hammerstein first wrote it, the child was to be a boy—no nonsense about a possible girl. Whereupon Rodgers, the aggrieved father of two daughters, arose in his wrath, sketched the music for an added section of the soliloquy, designed to discuss the possibility of a girl child's being born, and handed it to his partner with an indignant request to write words for it. Hammerstein obligingly complied. And a good thing he did. In *Carousel* as in *Liliom*, the child *is* a girl.

After a four-weeks' tryout in New Haven and Boston, *Carousel* opened at the Majestic Theatre in New York on the 170th anniversary of Paul Revere's ride—a coincidence that is of no significance whatsoever. There had been a little speculation as to how critics and audience would react to a musical comedy whose hero is killed halfway through the second act. There need not have been. *Carousel* had a re-

ception equaled only by that which had greeted *Oklahoma!*
The people of *Oklahoma!* were gay and real. *Carousel* ven-
tured to involve its people in a deep and touching love story.

The critics waxed lyrical. For John Chapman of the
*News,*

> "Carousel" is one of the finest musical plays I have ever seen,
> and I shall remember it always. It has everything the profes-
> sional theatre can give it and something besides: heart, integ-
> rity, an inner glow . . . tender . . . rueful, almost tragic. . . .
> Those looking for a happy and foolish evening had better go
> elsewhere.

The others were in a similar mood: "Fragile beauty and
an enchanting score . . . 'Carousel' becomes something
memorable in the theatre . . . touching and affecting . . .
something rare in the theatre" (Morehouse, the *Sun*); "This
'Carousel' for which I'm deliberately going off the deep end
. . . opened triumphantly . . . romantic, melodramatic, fan-
tastical, colorful, comic, tragic, melodic, and an evening of
sheer theatrical entertainment" (Garland, *Journal-American*); "a big, beautiful, beguiling musical" (Coleman,
*Mirror*); "on the whole, delightful . . . sometimes fast and
rousing, now nostalgic and moving" (Nichols, *Times*);
"definitely something to see . . . proved that music and real
drama can be combined outside the opera with very good
entertainment results" (Guernsey, Jr., *Herald Tribune*).

As in the case of *Oklahoma!* the exception to these rejoic-
ings came from the pen of Wilella Waldorf of the *Post*.
Miss Waldorf, who seems to have been definitely allergic
to Rodgers and Hammerstein, wrote that it "seemed a rather
long evening. The 'Oklahoma!' formula is becoming a bit

monotonous and so are Miss de Mille's ballets. All right, go ahead and shoot!"

No one accepted the invitation, but the public sided with the other critics. When *Carousel* finally closed, on May 24, 1947, its New York run, although necessarily dwarfed by the fantastic success of *Oklahoma!* had attained the healthy figure of 864 performances—two years and one month. Five days later, in Chicago, the company began a road tour that lasted twenty-one months. In June of 1950 a London company opened at the Drury Lane Theatre (where, some years before, *Liliom* had been a dire failure), and stayed for sixteen months. A road company is still touring England.

Again we revert to 1944. Having nothing to do—nothing creative, that is—beyond writing *Carousel*, they promptly signed a contract with Twentieth Century-Fox to provide the screenplay, lyrics, and music for *State Fair*, a remake of a story by Phil Stong that had been filmed in 1933. Their contract permitted them to do their work in New York, but Hammerstein agreed to go to the Coast, if necessary, to discuss possible changes with Walter Lang, the director of the picture. Shortly after the finished script had been delivered on the Coast, Hammerstein came down with what was thought to be appendicitis. He still looks back wistfully to his stay in the hospital; for during those two pleasant weeks he learned, first, that no changes in the *State Fair* script were needed; second, that *Oklahoma!* had been awarded a special Pulitzer Prize; and, third, that it wasn't appendicitis.

Twentieth Century gave *State Fair* a lavish production in technicolor, with a gilt-edged cast, reading like a Hollywood "Who's Who," that included Jeanne Crain, Dana Andrews, Dick Haymes, Vivian Blaine, Charles Winninger, Fay Bainter, and Donald Meek. It was released at the Roxy Theatre on August 30, 1945. The reviews were enthusiastic, the consensus being voiced by Archer Winsten of the *Post*, who observed that " 'State Fair' is to movie musicals what 'Oklahoma!' is to stage musicals. There is that same quality of a bright and wonderful morning." Of its six songs, three, "That's for Me," "It's a Grand Night for Singing," and "It Might as Well Be Spring," became immediate hits. The last-named received an Academy Award as the best original song. Altogether, *State Fair* was one of the most successful pictures of the year.

In the fall of 1945 Hammerstein joined forces with Jerome Kern in a revival of *Show Boat*. The rehearsals were saddened by the death of Kern, who had come East to help with the production and whose heart failed him on November 11. Hammerstein then took entire charge of the production, and the piece opened at the Ziegfeld Theatre on January 7, 1946. It played a year in New York, after which Rodgers joined Hammerstein in embarking it on a long road tour lasting a year and eight months.

Meanwhile, with *Show Boat* safely launched, the two started work on a new musical for the Theatre Guild. There was little preliminary fanfare regarding it. About all the curious could learn was that it would have an original story by Hammerstein and would bear the interesting —if not exactly informative—title of *Allegro*. Incidentally, the advance sale of tickets is rumored to have amounted to the astounding figure of $700,000.

The Guild presented it at the Majestic Theatre on October 10, 1947. It told the story of Dr. Joseph Taylor, Jr., from his birth, through college and medical school, to his lucrative practice as a fashionable physician, and at the last, his disgust at the shallowness and neuroticism of his wealthy patients, and his abandonment of the city and return to the small town from which he had come.

The critical reception was mixed. Barnes of the *Herald Tribune* registered an emphatic yes: "A musical play of rare distinction." So did Coleman of the *Mirror*: "Great new musical . . . a stunning blending of beauty, integrity, intelligence, imagination, taste, and skill." Likewise Morehouse of the *Sun*: "Excitingly unconventional in form."

Others said yes and no. Thus Atkinson, of the *Times*: "For at least half its length, it is a work of great purity and beauty . . . until the disaster of 1929 overtakes it, 'Allegro' has the lyric rapture of a musical masterpiece." Watts of the *Post* was cautious: "A distinguished musical play. I have certain reservations about it, but there is no disputing the fact that it is a notable achievement in its field." Likewise Garland of the *Journal-American*: " 'Allegro' went its slow, unhurried way, telling a simple run-of-the-U.S.A. biography . . . suffers from over-elaboration . . . bigger than anything Rodgers and Hammerstein have written."

Chapman of the *News* called it "an elaborate sermon by two serious showmen," while Hawkins of the *World-Telegram* pulled no punches: "A vast disappointment. It lacks consistency of mood, visual excitement, and theatrical stimulation."

It seems a little foolish to call a musical play that ran

forty weeks in New York and thirty-one on the road a failure. *Allegro's* New York run was only three weeks shorter than that of *Music in the Air*, seven weeks *longer* than that of *A Connecticut Yankee*, and eleven weeks longer than that of *Jumbo*—all three of which had been considered hits. But if it was not a failure it was definitely not a success, by Rodgers and Hammerstein standards. For one thing, the production was elaborate and costly; and despite Donaldson Awards for the season's best book, lyrics, and music, the customers simply did not attend in sufficient numbers to repay the investment. The authors and the Guild were understandably disappointed, although the blow must have been softened by contemplating *Oklahoma!* then entering its sixth year in New York. Besides, Rodgers and Hammerstein had other fish to fry.

In January, 1942, James A. Michener, a teacher and editor of textbooks for the Macmillan Company, joined the Navy and was assigned to duty in the South Pacific. Exactly three years later he found himself on a small island with nothing in particular to do except observe his fellow men—and women. He had always wanted to write, and here were both the opportunity and the material. Grasping the one, he embodied the other in a series of sketches about the people who were spending the war in the Pacific. Early that summer he mailed the manuscript to the Macmillan Company, using an assumed name so that he would not seem to be trading on his former position. Macmillan liked the book, and suggested certain cuts and alterations, which were duly made.

Everything happens in January to Michener. In January, 1946, he was discharged from the Navy and went back to his old job at Macmillan's. In January, 1947, *Tales of the South Pacific* was published, and received the Pulitzer Price for fiction. The book sold about 25,000 copies in its first year—not a phenomenal sale, but a satisfying one.

An advance copy had been sent to Kenneth MacKenna, a former actor who was head of the story department of Metro-Goldwyn-Mayer. He liked it, and thought it had the makings of a good picture; but M-G-M did nothing about it. About a year later, early in 1948, when he was at supper with his brother, Jo Mielziner, and Joshua Logan, respectively the scene designer and coauthor and director of *Mister Roberts*, then in production, he mentioned the book, suggesting that they read it. Logan did so, was struck with its dramatic possibilities, and took it to Leland Hayward, the producer of *Mister Roberts*. Hayward was equally impressed; and together they entered into an informal agreement with Michener to make a play based on the stories.

Logan, in turn, mentioned the book to Rodgers, who mentioned it to Hammerstein. Together they read it, and pounced upon it as material for a musical play. Following the production of *Allegro* they had made a pact that in the future they would produce as well as write their musical plays. Accordingly, they made an agreement with Logan and Hayward whereby the dramatic rights to the *Tales* were assigned to them: they to write book, lyrics, and music, and produce the piece, with Logan as director, and he and Hayward as coproducers.

That settled, all that remained was for Rodgers and Hammerstein to write the piece. They began with a negative approach: owing to the realistic atmosphere of the stories, there would be no ballet. For dramatic purposes, two of the stories seemed outstanding: "Fo' Dollah," describing the love of Lieutenant Cable for Liat, the daughter of a disreputable old native woman known as Bloody Mary; and "Our Heroine," concerning Nurse Nellie Forbush and her love for the middle-aged French planter De Becque. One problem, that of the chorus, was easily solved: nurses and Seabees. But who was to be the hero, and how were the two stories to be combined? Furthermore, one of the most attractive characters in the book, named Tony Fry, appeared in two or three of the tales, and was obvious leading-man material—but he didn't appear in either "Fo' Dollah" or "Our Heroine." Finally, after upward of four months of story conferences, they threw Fry out and made De Becque the hero.

This decision was hastened by a trip that they made to Los Angeles, to see a traveling company of *Annie Get Your Gun*, headed by Mary Martin. While there, they learned that the glamorous Ezio Pinza, the great basso of the Metropolitan, was available for a picture or a play. In June of 1948 he came East for a broadcast. The partners took him to lunch, accompanied him to the broadcast, heard him sing before the studio audience, and signed him up. Having taken one plunge, they decided to take another, telephoned to Mary Martin in San Francisco, and offered her the part of Nellie Forbush. Miss Martin's reaction, upon learning that she was supposed to sing opposite Pinza, was to inquire, anxiously, as to their sanity. However, when she returned East, she was lured to the Rodgers summer home in Fairfield, Connecticut, where Logan read the first twelve pages of the script and Rodgers played the first four numbers of the score. They had no further trouble with her.

The problem of combining the De Becque-Forbush and Cable-Liat stories was solved by sending the two men together on a dangerous mission—from which one was destined not to return. Tired of hearing countless puns on *Tales*, they shortened the title to *South Pacific* and started rehearsals on February 2, 1949. In contrast to the weary round of auditions that had preceded the production of *Oklahoma!* the $225,000 that *South Pacific* cost was raised by the simple expedient of allowing prospective backers to invest. The advance sale of tickets, while not up to the $700,000 that ushered in *Allegro*, was still a by no means beggarly half-million.

On March 7 the Company opened a trial run of four weeks in New Haven and Boston. Even during rehearsals the rumors began to float about that *South Pacific* was something to look forward to, and scouts who attended the dress rehearsal in New Haven rushed back to New York wide-eyed.

On April 7, 1949, *South Pacific* opened in New York at the Majestic Theatre. There is no need to quote here what all of the reviewers had to say about it. Three will suffice. Brooks Atkinson, of the *Times*, called it "a magnificent musical drama . . . rhapsodically enjoyable . . . a tenderly beautiful idyll of genuine people inexplicably tossed together in a strange corner of the world . . . as lively, warm, fresh, and beautiful as we had all hoped that it would be." Richard Watts, of the *Post*, wrote, "An utterly captivating work of theatrical art . . . a work of great style and loveliness that is yet gay, vigorous, and vital . . . both strangely touching and richly entertaining . . . the rarest and most tasteful showmanship." According to a British visitor, Frederick Cook, of the London *Evening Standard*, "The only thing to do is take off one's hat, borrow an expressive old Americanism, and say 'Wow!'" The others said the same things in different words. The verdict was unanimous.

There has never been anything quite to equal the demand for tickets to *South Pacific* that followed. It may have been caused by the reviews, or the reputation of Rodgers and Hammerstein, or the magic names of Martin and Pinza, or old-fashioned word-of-mouth—probably all four. Whatever the reason, people simply had to see, and hear, the story of Nellie and De Becque. The scalpers had a field day. It has been estimated that the audience at a given performance has actually paid about four times the box office price. Tickets were given as bribes—one man known to this correspondent offered his income tax collector three pairs, for which he had paid a tidy hundred dollars apiece. (Whether or not the outraged collector accepted them I wouldn't know.)

Possessing tickets to *South Pacific* actually became a mark of social distinction. Persons who hadn't seen the show begged ticket stubs from their more fortunate neighbors in order to deposit them negligently on the mantelpiece for the edification of dinner guests. The backers had their money back after the first four months. The sales of sheet music are well over the two million mark. Over *one million* record albums have been issued—and sold.

It is hardly necessary to add that the show annexed just about all the awards in sight, including the New York Drama Critics' Circle award for the best musical play of 1949-50; the Antoinette Perry Awards (in eight categories) for 1949-50; the Donaldson Awards (nine categories) for 1948-49; and the Pulitzer Prize Drama Award for 1950.

As this book goes to press, *South Pacific* is still running in New York. It still plays to capacity at virtually every performance, its solid entertainment qualities being eloquently attested by the fact that it has had three Nellie Forbushes and four De Becques—with nobody demanding his money back. One can only guess as to how much longer it will run. Suppose we take an arbitrary date: January 1, 1954. At that time *South Pacific* will have played 1,971 performances—four years, nine months, and two weeks—with only 231 performances to go before it equals the New York run of *Oklahoma!* It will have been seen by upward of 3,150,000 persons, and will have grossed something over $11,500,000. Tickets are still being sold for weeks ahead.

By that same date, January 1, 1954, a second company, which went on the road on April 24, 1950, will have been returning substantial profits for a little over three years and eight months. A London company, which opened at Drury Lane on November 1, 1951, a company in Australia and another in Denmark, both of which opened on September 8, 1952, are still running.

Margaret Landon's book, *Anna and the King of Siam,*

190

tells the story (a true one) of Anna Leonowens, a widowed mid-Victorian lady who arrived in the 1860's at the court of the king of Siam to be the teacher of the royal children. The theme of the story concerns the crisis she met, in the classroom and in connection with the king's affairs, and the influence she bore on the destiny of an Oriental nation still unaffected by Western civilization. Sometime in the late forties the two Dorothys—Rodgers and Hammerstein—had read the book, and had seen in it the possibilities of a musical play. They submitted this idea to their respective lords and masters, who firmly rejected it. Sometime later Gertrude Lawrence made a similar suggestion, and in return received a figurative rejection slip. Still later, a literary agent laid the book on the Rodgers and Hammerstein desk. By this time the partners had seen the film version of *Anna* and had drastically revised their opinion as to its stage possibilities.

Not only was it an absorbing story and a most unusual one, but it was a challenge to both; and they like challenges. Their four previous plays had been all-American in setting, in costumes, in plot, and in speech (granted that the locale of *South Pacific* is not technically American, the all-American personnel makes it temporarily so). In *Anna* Hammerstein had to fashion a book and lyrics from a story laid in a foreign country, and an Oriental country at that, with a cast of which only four roles were Anglo-Saxon.

Rodgers had his problem, too: that of writing a score that would suggest an Oriental atmosphere without overdoing it. In his own words, "It seems certain that a too-accurate reproduction of the sound of 1860 Siam would give less than small pleasure to the Occidental ear, and an evening of it would drive an American audience howling into the streets. . . . I finally decided to write a score that would be analogous, in sound, to the look of a series of Siamese paintings by Grant Wood."

On the night of February 26, 1951, following the world première of *Anna and the King of Siam*, rechristened *The King and I* (the partners have a wonderful flair for good titles) at the Shubert Theatre in New Haven, Connecticut, there happened something not far from unique in American theatrical history. The Rodgers and the Hammersteins went to Kaysey's Restaurant for an after-theater supper and celebration. The book, the lyrics, John van Druten's direction, Jo Mielziner's beautiful sets and lighting, Irene Sharaff's equally lovely costumes, Jerome Robbins' choreography —all made an irresistible combination. The piece was forty-five minutes too long; but cutting is easy. There was nothing to rewrite, nothing to add, no new songs to put in, no others to take out. No sitting up all night in a hotel room. The audience had applauded, and laughed, and wept in all the right places. The show was "in."

All of the above, a digest of what was related to me by an excited alleged eyewitness, is a sterling example of the fact that while truth may be stranger than fiction, fiction is a lot more fun. Mr. Hammerstein's only comment on the tale just related was to remark, dryly, that while his recollection of the after-theater party was imperfect, he did recollect that three important songs, "Getting to Know You," "I Have Dreamed," and "Western People Funny," were written and added to the score during the last week in Boston. And two others were taken out.

Ah, well. A pity it wasn't true.

*The King and I* played to packed houses for a week in New Haven and three weeks in Boston. It opened in New York at the St. James Theatre on March 29, 1951. In the critical reaction to it there was a certain amount of a word that I have been trying to use for thirty years: ambivalence.[1] Brooks Atkinson, of the *Times*, and Richard Watts, of the *Post*, rather bewilderingly gave with one hand and took away with the other. According to Atkinson:

"The King and I" is no match for "South Pacific." . . . Strictly on its terms . . . an original and beautiful excursion into the rich splendors of the Far East, done with impeccable taste by two artists, and brought to life with a warm, romantic score, idiomatic lyrics, and some exquisite dancing. . . . Don't expect another "South Pacific" or an "Oklahoma!"

Likewise Watts:

A beautiful and fascinating musical play, a splendid successor to the great "South Pacific." It has color, beauty, and a strange kind of sweetness, a good story, characteristically fine music and lyrics. . . . Unfairly but inevitably everyone will want to know if it is as good as "South Pacific." I will confess that I don't suppose it is. But what is?

John Chapman, of the *News*, and Robert Coleman, of the *Mirror*, both mentioned its distinguished predecessor, but admitted no comparison. Thus Chapman:

Is it as good as "South Pacific" or "Oklahoma!"? All I can answer is that there is no sense in asking for a comparison, for

---

[1] "Simultaneous attraction toward and repulsion from an object, person, or action."—*Webster's Unabridged.*

"The King and I" is something different . . . an intricate and expert piece of showmanship in which the story comes first.

Coleman wrote:

It has heart, drama, comedy, and eye-filling spectacle. . . . "The King and I" sets a new high standard for the musical stage. We see no reason to compare it with Rodgers and Hammerstein's fabulous "South Pacific." . . . It is an event not to be missed.

John Lardner, in *The New Yorker*, pronounced it a draw:

"The touches of character drawing . . . and its faithfulness to a reasonably adult and literate story, make this at least as novel and effective a musical, for my taste, as "South Pacific."

There were no signs of ambivalence about the rest, although one or two were less than paroxysmic: " 'The King and I' has not the masterpiece's brilliance, but it glows with its own softer lights of consistent entertainment" (Guernsey, *Herald Tribune*). "The boys have done it again. . . . There is not the slightest doubt that they have another big hit for them . . . not a great score according to Richard Rodgers' standards" (McClain, *Journal-American*).

The others were old-fashioned raves: "A stunning show, taste, style, and singular beauty . . . something I shall be going back to see for all of the next decade" (Morehouse, *World-Telegram*). "The music acts on the story in much the same way that technicolor does to a moving picture; it is not so much an addition as it is an illumination of the play" (Hawkins, *World-Telegram*). "Different from the rest . . . lyrical and handsome and adult as always, and sometimes as legitimately dramatic as a play . . . it is a musical like nothing you have ever seen before, dappled with many delights" (Pollack, *Compass*). "The most enchanting thing in New York . . . a score of size, of melodious reaches that are piercingly emotional and satisfying in the most demanding degree" (Bolton, *Morning Telegraph*).

Writing in his daily column in the *News*, Danton Walker found something in the music that the others had missed:

With the launching of "The King and I" Rodgers and Hammerstein could well retire and rest on their laurels; for here is one of the most distinguished productions of this or any other season. . . . It may not be Dick Rodgers' most popular score, but with arranger Russell Bennett's assist, it is certainly his best, musically speaking

—a shrewd and penetrating verdict, of which more anon. Incidentally, a few nights after the opening, Brooks Atkinson, at the invitation of Rodgers and Hammerstein, saw the performance again, and had all the ambivalence knocked out of him. His article in the *Times*, the following Sunday, was another for the rave column.

Seven months after *The King* had opened, there was staged a revival of Hammerstein and Kern's 1933 success, *Music in the Air*. For some reason it had little success, the blame probably resting upon the shoulders of Rodgers and Hammerstein, whose *Oklahoma! Carousel*, *Allegro*, *South Pacific*, and *The King and I*, in their realism, had dealt a death blow to the conventional operetta formula.

Rodgers had better luck. On January 3, 1952, Jule Styne and Leonard Key revived *Pal Joey* at the Broadhurst Theatre, where it proved to be as emphatic a success as it had been ten years before. Brooks Atkinson, of the *Times*, had written of the 1941 production, "The ugly topic that is up for discussion stands between the theater-goer and real enjoyment of a well-staged show." In '52 he ate a small portion of boiled crow:

There was a minority in 1941, including this column, that was not enchanted. But no one is likely now to be impervious to the tight organization of the production, the terseness of the writing, the liveliness and versatility of the score, and the easy perfection of the lyrics.

When *Pal Joey* closed in New York on April 18, 1953, it had enjoyed a run (one year and four months) two months longer than that of the 1941 production. *The King and I* is still with us. The length of its probable run is, of course, a matter of pure guesswork. Suffice it to say that by New Year's of 1954 it will have run 640 performances (two years and eight months), with tickets on sale twelve weeks ahead. By acting quickly you can probably get two good seats for some evening next April.

Composer Rodgers and lyrist Hammerstein look unworried watching a rehearsal of *Oklahoma!*, with reason. The show opened at the St. James Theatre on March 31, 1943 and ran for 2,202 performances in New York. (Photo by John Swope.)

Bambi Lynn dances in one of Agnes de Mille's ballets, which contributed greatly to the success of *Oklahoma!* (Courtesy of The Theatre Guild.)

The cast of *Oklahoma!* around the Surrey with the Fringe on Top. Lee Dixon, as Will Parker who sang "Kansas City" is next to Celeste Holm, while Alfred Drake as Curly sits in the surrey with Joan Roberts as Laurey. (Courtesy of The Theatre Guild.)

At the 2,001st performance of *Oklahoma!*, Fiorello La Guardia, above, is on stage with the cast and Lawrence Langner, Oscar Hammerstein and Richard Rodgers. Below, these honorary Oklahoman Indian chiefs are, from left to right; Oscar Hammerstein, Lawrence Langner, Richard Rodgers, Mrs. Lawrence Langner, Agnes de Mille and Theresa Helburn.

These two pictures illustrate the liveliness and vigor of Agnes de Mille's choreography for *Carousel*. Also a Theatre Guild production, it ran at the Majestic Theatre from April, 1945, to May, 1947. (Courtesy of Oscar Hammerstein II.)

A Happy Birthday Party for the composer and lyrist of *Oklahoma!* and *Carousel*.

*Allegro*, which opened in October, 1947, was not a success by Rodgers and Hammerstein standards, although it ran for forty weeks in New York and thirty-one on the road. The critics viewed it more favorably than the customers, although one of the former described it as "an elaborate sermon," the story of a fashionable city doctor, who renounces his neurotic, wealthy patients to return to practice in his small home town. The picture shows the cast of *Allegro*. (Courtesy of Oscar Hammerstein II.)

Richard Rodgers composes the music for one of the loveliest songs from *South Pacific*, "Bali Ha'i." *South Pacific* opened at the Majestic Theatre on April 7, 1949, and, in contrast to *Allegro*, the critics and the customers were unanimous in their approval. (Photo by John Swope.)

Mary Martin played Nellie Forbush, a Navy nurse. Here she entertains the men by singing "Honey Bun." (Courtesy of Oscar Hammerstein II.)

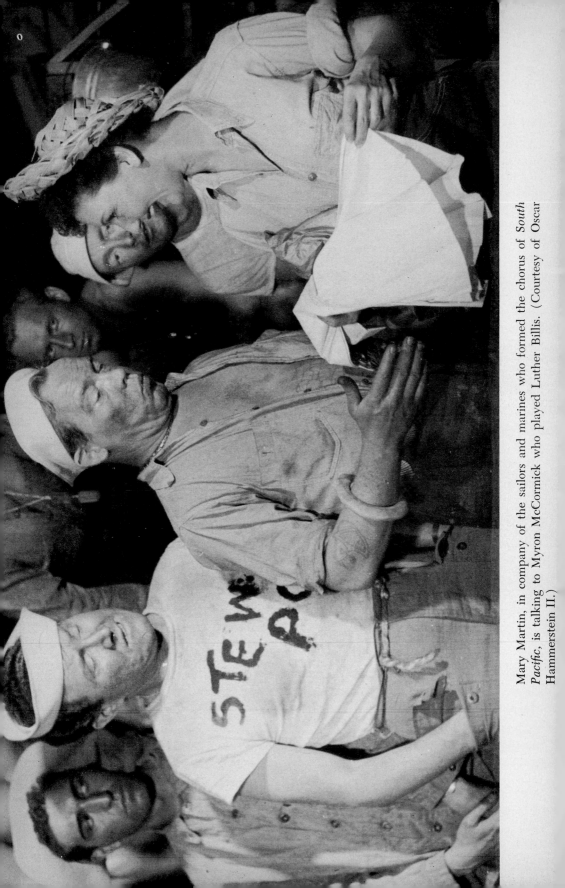

Mary Martin, in company of the sailors and marines who formed the chorus of *South Pacific*, is talking to Myron McCormick who played Luther Billis. (Courtesy of Oscar Hammerstein II.)

Ezio Pinza as Emile de Becque was one of the greatest attractions of the show. Here he is with Mary Martin and his two children, Ngana and Jerome, who opened *South Pacific* with the song "Dites-moi pourquoi." (Courtesy of Oscar Hammerstein II.)

Some of the personalities involved in *South Pacific*, both on stage and off. Above, left to right, the composer, Joshua Logan, who staged it, Hammerstein and Leland Hayward, co-producer. Below, left to right, Oscar Hammerstein, Mrs. Ezio Pinza, Ezio Pinza, Dorothy Hammerstein, Dorothy Rodgers and the composer.

Taken by Joshua Logan, this picture, right, shows Hammerstein and Rodgers working on the book and score of the *The King and I*. Below, after a successful Boston opening, the authors relax on the Boston Common. (Photo by Hy Peskin.) *The King and I*, based on Margaret Landon's *Anna and the King of Siam*, opened in New York on March 29, 1951, again to become an immediate success. It was the first musical done by the collaborators that did not have an all-American setting.

Yul Brynner on stage with his many wives and children, as befits an Oriental monarch. Gertrude Lawrence adds a Western touch to the setting in her Victorian garb. (Courtesy of Oscar Hammerstein II.)

The two principals of *The King and I*, Gertrude Lawrence as Anna, the governess, and Yul Brynner as the King, together in a dance choreographed by Jerome Robbins. (Courtesy of Oscar Hammerstein II.)

Sixth of Rodgers and Hammerstein shows is *Me and Juliet*, which opened in New York on May 28, 1953. A play within a play, it is Rodgers' and Hammerstein's tribute to the love of their lives, the theater. This picture shows Joan McCracken in a dance designed by Robert Alton. (Photo by Eileen Darby.)

# Part Four

Some fifteen years ago, a reporter, in the course of an interview with Oscar Hammerstein II, wrote that he looked like a construction foreman. About five years later, another reporter, in the course of an interview with Oscar Hammerstein II, likewise wrote that he looked like a construction foreman. About five years later, a third reporter, in the course of an interview with Oscar Hammerstein II, gave him a promotion, remarking that he looked like a construction *engineer*. It is customary, in the course of interviews with Richard Rodgers, to remark that he looks like a family doctor (his brother, whom he strongly resembles, is a famous obstetrician) or a stockbroker. In other words, unless a man happens to look like Beethoven or Goethe, he is supposed not to look like a musician or a poet.

Hammerstein is something over six feet tall, heavy-set —"burly," I think, would be the word—craggy-looking, with an air that is deceptively easygoing. Rodgers is shorter —"stocky" would be *his* word—still in possession of most of his hair, although a bit talcumed, with an air rather taut and energetic. Both men were born and brought up in the same environment (uptown New York), both went to Columbia University, and have strikingly similar tastes. Hammerstein doesn't smoke, and drinks sparingly. Ditto, Rodgers. Hammerstein has a five-story house in East Sixty-third Street; Rodgers has a duplex apartment on upper Park Avenue. Hammerstein has a country house and farm near Doylestown, Pennsylvania, where he raises Black Angus cattle. Rodgers has a country house near Southport, Connecticut, where he has established the world's largest croquet ground. Both have maintained about the same standard of living for twenty-five years. Both spent some unhappy years in Hollywood. Furthermore, in a burst of unanimity that seems a little excessive, each has a wife named Dorothy who is an interior decorator.

On your left as you enter the ground-floor entrance foyer of the Hammerstein town house is a door, papered to match the walls. It would be invisible except for a sign which reads: HAMMERSTEIN OFFICE—MARY STEELE, SEC. —TURN KNOB—COME IN. It is here that his secretary attends to his private correspondence and types his scripts from dictaphone records. The use of this instrument he picked up from Joshua Logan, when they were working together on *South Pacific*. Says Miss Steele, simply, "He adores it." He dictates everything except his lyrics, which he writes in longhand. He does this, he explains, because if they were typewritten they would look so perfect that he wouldn't have the heart to make any changes.

His working habits are those that you might expect from a construction foreman—pardon, engineer—rather than from a poet. He rises at eight, has breakfast at eight-thirty, and is at his desk at nine.

The one place to which he never goes, if he can possibly avoid it, is the Rodgers and Hammerstein office on Madison Avenue, which he regards with simple loathing. This is Rodgers' domain. What with guiding the fortunes of their musical plays—five of which are still very active— to say nothing of their activities as play producers, Rodgers and Hammerstein are decidedly Big Business. And Rodgers takes an active hand in that business whenever he is in New York. The office force now numbers nine, including his personal secretary, an office manager, a casting director, a librarian, a receptionist, and assistants, and even when he is not actually in the office he keeps in constant touch, telephoning in, or leaving telephone numbers where he can be found at any hour. All this leaves Hammerstein a little wide-eyed, his conclusion being that "he must like it, or he wouldn't be doing it." The probable truth is that even when he is working on a new play, he composes so swiftly that he is left with a good deal of extra time on his hands; and the office offers a ready outlet for his surplus energy. One project that he is directing at present is the formation of a complete library of the scripts and orchestrations of the Rodgers and Hart shows, the Rodgers and Hammerstein shows, and the show, written with other composers, of which Hammerstein was the author in whole or in part. This is easier said than done, for the material for some of the older shows has been so long forgotten that it has simply disappeared; and digging it up necessitates a wearisome amount of research.

The office is a pleasant place to visit. The staff obviously like their jobs, and like and admire their bosses. About the only complaint one hears is that Hammerstein doesn't come around often enough. Not that they want to put him to work; they just want to see him.

This attitude is pretty generally shared along Broadway. The two have a reputation for kindliness and hospitality that is rare among authors and producers. Unlike some of their contemporaries, they have not forgotten their own youthful struggles, and make a point of finding and encouraging new talent. Joan Roberts and Alfred Drake, for example, were comparative unknowns when they were engaged for the leading roles in *Oklahoma!*

When they are casting a show, anyone can get an audition, and will be given a serious hearing. Many of the youthful applicants arrive, of course, scared to death, and don't do themselves justice. They are likely to forget words, run out of breath, sing flat. When some trembling neophyte shows signs of cracking up, Rodgers will remark, cheerfully: "Wait a minute. Now just relax for a little while and then try again. We've never shot anybody yet." If a candidate shows up who seems particularly promising, but for whom they have no suitable part, Rodgers is not above telephoning to another producer, to recommend that he give the newcomer a hearing.

Things are different, of course, when the partners are working on a new show of their own. Then Rodgers is seen at the office only occasionally, Hammerstein not at all. They meet at each other's homes—in New York or in the country—for an endless series of conferences, discussing the story line, the musical numbers, just where they should go, just what the mood of a given number should be. This goes on for weeks, sometimes for months, before Hammerstein goes to the dictaphone or Rodgers picks up a sheet of music paper.

They use music as much as possible. I mentioned before the way in which the basic musical numbers in *Oklahoma!* were woven into the story. This became increasingly true of their subsequent scores.

When the conductor of a musical play rises from his chair at a given moment of the score, raises his baton, and starts the orchestra, that, in show parlance, is a music cue. The score of *Oklahoma!* comprised only twelve basic numbers, but called for twenty-nine such music cues. That of *Carousel* contains thirteen numbers and thirty-one music cues; *Allegro*, sixteen numbers and forty-four cues; *South Pacific*, fifteen numbers, forty-nine cues; *The King and I*, sixteen numbers, forty-six cues. In other words, in a play such as *The King and I*, even when there is no singing, there is a well-nigh continuous murmur of music, whether under dialogue or to illustrate a scene in pantomime. It is a device that greatly helps the plausibility of the action and eases immeasurably the transition from speech to song.

Theirs is a collaboration far more complete than is the case with many other words-and-music partnerships. Rodgers has a very keen dramatic sense, and a fine literary taste. He writes charmingly himself—if he is not a professional writer it is only because he does not choose to be one. Hammerstein, on the other hand, has great understanding of music; thus the two see eye to eye as regards musical and dramatic values. Another feature of their collaboration that has produced the happiest results is the manner in which their words and music are combined. During his entire career with Lorenz Hart, Rodgers followed the traditional Broadway practice of writing the music first and then handing the tune to the lyrist to find words to go with it. Hammerstein, up to the time when he started work with Rodgers, had followed the same method—writing words to go with tunes that were handed to him.

The two now reverse the process. Hammerstein writes a lyric and gives it to Rodgers to set to the music; an infinitely better system—provided the composer is capable of following it. Under the current Broadway system the music imposes its will upon the words—creating the emotion and then inventing the sense—a method that frequently produces all too awkward results. As Rodgers and Hammerstein work, the lyrist is set free to use his imagination, to experiment with new forms and rhythms, to develop his ideas logically instead of bending them to the demands of the music. To the composer, such lyrics are a challenge and a release, testing his inventive powers and at the same time offering him new rhythms and forms that he might not have thought of, working "cold."

For example: Suppose Rodgers had handed Hammerstein the tune of "It Might as Well Be Spring." Even granted that they had agreed upon the title beforehand, would the words have been those we hear now? Would Rodgers have thought of the music for "Many a New Day," with its provocative triplets, if he had not had Hammerstein's lyric before him? Or—one more—would Rodgers have evolved a longish number with the following successive time signatures: 2/2; 6/8; 2/4; 6/8; 2/4; 6/8; 2/2 —if he had not read Hammerstein's lyric for "I'm Gonna

Wash That Man Right Outa My Hair"? I take leave to doubt it.

One amusing reminder of Hammerstein's old setting-words-to-music days links him with the late Rudyard Kipling. The latter, in writing his *Barrack Room Ballads,* avowedly set them to the rhythms of popular songs of his day. Hammerstein, when he sets out to write a lyric, hums it to a tune of his own devising. He is frequently disconcerted to discover that Rodgers' tune for that lyric turns out to be something quite different—and better.

Rodgers, when he sets to work, composes with incredible speed. I once asked him (discovering, later, that others had asked the same question) how long it took him to write "Oh, What a Beautiful Mornin'."

His reply was, "How long does it take to play it?" He was not being smart-aleck. He seldom takes more than a day, or even an hour or so, to set any lyric to music. Remember, however, those preliminary conferences. "By the time Oscar gave me the lyrics," he says, "and I sat down to the actual business of writing the notes, I already knew all the governing circumstances—the scene, the mood, the singer, the subject, and even the fact that it was to be a waltz, a simple little waltz. These things had all been decided."

When he composes, he concentrates until the score is finished. He writes his own piano arrangements. While he does not do the actual orchestration of his shows (rehearsals and tryout changes make that impracticable), he gives the arranger—usually Russell Bennett—an orchestral sketch that embodies his ideas as to the instrumentation.

Once a score is finished, he hibernates, musically, until the next one. During these blank periods he holds curiously aloof from music. He is not a great concertgoer, he goes to the opera only occasionally, and may not touch the piano for weeks at a time. I have heard him quoted as saying that if he wished, he could probably write a song a day, the year around.

As to that I am a bit skeptical, being inclined to think that even if he could, they would not (how to word it politely?) all be of equal excellence. He is primarily a man of the theater, and he needs the stimulus of the theater to do his best work. The so-called "blank" periods are probably periods of lying fallow, necessary intervals in which to store up musical energy for the next task.

Hammerstein, on the contrary, writes very slowly, testing and retesting until he has written something that satisfies him. He is a little plaintive over the fact that it may take him three weeks to write a lyric that Rodgers sets to music in three hours. He brings one invaluable gift to the lyric theater—due partly to the fact that he writes both book and lyrics: His songs are written in the language of the spoken dialogue, so that the transition, in one of their plays, from speech to song is so smooth as to be as nearly imperceptible as such a thing could be. Incidentally, he has a quaint hankering for dialect. Look at the list:

*Carmen Jones,* Negro dialect; *Oklahoma!,* Western; *Carousel,* New England. *South Pacific,* while perhaps not technically written in dialect, is couched in Army and Navy lingo, which is almost a dialect in itself, and one character speaks with a French accent. *The King and I* is written in

English that most of the characters speak with an exotic accent. The only exception, thus far, is *Allegro*.

Hammerstein is something of a phenomenon, a writer of Broadway musicals who is a poet. His lyrics have a beautiful simplicity and directness, great warmth and sincerity of emotion, and a love and understanding of simple people. How exactly right, for instance, are these lines from *Oklahoma!* sung by a cowboy who is taking his girl home from a dance:

> The sun is swimmin' on the rim of a hill,
>    The moon is takin' a header,
> And jist as I'm thinkin' all the earth is still,
>    A lark'll wake up in the medder. . . .
> Hush! You bird, my baby's a-sleepin'—
> May be got a dream worth a-keepin'. . . .
> Whoa! You team, and jist keep a-creepin'
> At a slow clip-clop;
> Don't you hurry with the surrey
> With the fringe on the top.

Curly knows what he feels, and he would say it just that way.

Hammerstein has said that when he began work on *Oklahoma!* he knew he could write the sentimental and vigorous lyrics, but was worried about writing the comic ones. That he need not have worried is testified, for instance by "Kansas City," "I Cain't Say No," or by "All er Nothin'."

Inevitably, there are those who want to know how Lorenz Hart and Hammerstein compare. Which was the better? To me, the works of the two men live in separate worlds. You can compare Hart with W. S. Gilbert, but not with Hammerstein. Suppose we take a simple situation —two young people about to go to a new home, and see how each treats it. Thus Hart, from the *Second Garrick Gaieties*:

When the world was young,
Old Father Adam with sin would grapple,
So we're entitled to just one apple,
   I mean to make apple sauce.
Underneath the bough
We'll learn a lesson from Mister Omar;
Beneath the eyes of no Pa and no Ma(r).
   Old Lady Nature is boss.
Washing dishes,
Catching fishes
   In the running stream,
We'll curse the smell a'
Citronella
   Even when we dream.
Head upon the ground
Your downy pillow is just a boulder.
I'll have new dimples before I'm older;
But life is peaches and cream.
And if you're good,
I'll search for wood,
So you can cook
While I stand look-
ing.
Beans could get no keener re-
Ception in a beanery.
Bless our mountain greenery
home.

Here is Hammerstein on the same subject:

When I marry Mister Snow,
The flowers will be buzzin' with the hum of bees,
    The birds'll make a racket in the churchyard trees,
When I marry Mister Snow.

Then it's off to home we go,
    And both of us will look a little dreamy-eyed,
    A-drivin' to a cottage by the ocean side,
Where the salty breezes blow.

He'll carry me across the threshold,
And I'll be as meek as a lamb.
    Then he'll set me on my feet,
    And I'll say, kinda sweet,
"Well, Mister Snow, here I am!"

Obviously the two have nothing in common. Hart's young people are brash city kids, true enough. But the difference between them and Carrie Pipperidge is the difference between their creators. Hart's rhymes are incredibly ingenious, and the lines are always gay. They crackle and sparkle. He is obviously greatly concerned about the manner in which he says his say. But Hammerstein's lyric has a quiet glow, an unconscious poetry that is the work of an artist who is concerned with *what* he has to say. Hart has brilliance. Hammerstein has simplicity. Both are admirable—and incomparable.

His rhymes are so apparently effortless that one is almost unconscious of them, so natural do they sound. Take this stanza from *Oklahoma!*:

> Never gonna think that the man I lose
>     Is the only man among men.
> I'll snap my fingers to show I don't care,
> I'll buy me a brand-new dress to wear.
> I'll scrub my neck and I'll bresh my hair,
>     And start all over again!

He has an odd gift for writing in what one might call a vein of humorous tenderness—like this, from *Carousel*:

> A-rockin' upon the sea,
> Your boat will seem to be
>     Like a dear little baby in her bassinet,
> For she hasn't learned to walk,
> And she hasn't learned to talk,
>     And her little behind
>     Is kind of inclined to be wet!

—or this, from the same play:

> But my little girl gets hungry ev'ry night,
> And she comes home to me.

He can create a mood in six lines, such as these, from *Oklahoma!*:

> The floor creaks,
> The door squeaks,
>     There's a field mouse a-nibblin' on a broom;
> And I set by myself
> Like a cobweb on a shelf,
>     By myself in a lonely room.

Every once in a while he makes a neat metaphor:

A chrysanthemum spout come out of the snout of a whale.

—or writes a sudden, stabbing little phrase of pure poetry:

> It's a grand night for singing,
> The moon is flying high,
> And somewhere a bird that is bound he'll be heard
> Is throwing his heart at the sky.

What luck for Rodgers!

One of the most striking things about Rodgers' music is his extraordinary versatility. He can handle any dance form—waltzes, fox trots, tangos, mazurkas, polkas, hornpipes—all with equal facility and apparent ease. He can handle a sentimental mood, a serious one, or a comic one. Since his association with Hammerstein he has gained greatly in dramatic power, and, rising to the challenge of his partner's variety in lyrics, has written music in many unorthodox forms (the old-fashioned sixteen-bar verse and thirty-two-bar chorus is now the exception in his music).

One characteristic phase of his work is his ability to make tunes out of repeated notes—an almost unique gift. Just how he does it is difficult to say. Just why should a song from *Oklahoma!* that begins like this:

be instantly recognizable? And why should my favorite waltz start off like this:

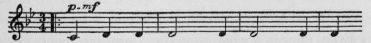

—and be captivating, whereas by all the rules of sensible melody-writing it ought to be monotonous? Or take one of the hit numbers in *The King and I* as "I Whistle a Happy Tune." Miss Gertrude Lawrence[1] began with a shower of repeated notes:

—and a little later had this to contribute:

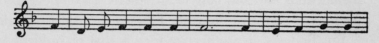

Who called that a tune? But it is. As the king of Siam himself remarks, it's a puzzlement.

Another feature of his music is his very sparing use of elaborate harmonies. When he needs them, he has them, and handles them with enormous skill. But as a rule, he gets along without them as long as he can. Here are the opening measures of two of his hit songs. First comes "People Will Say We're in Love" from *Oklahoma!*:

And here is "June Is Bustin' Out All Over," from *Carousel*:

The first group of notes needs only a tonic chord of D-major for its accompaniment, the second, a tonic chord of A-major. He has one harmonic trick, however, that is vastly effective. That is, to add a sort of extracurricular note to

[1] Miss Lawrence died on September 6, 1952. Miss Constance Carpenter, who had been her understudy, replaced her.

another mild and inoffensive chord—such as this phrase from *Me and Juliet*:

The resultant dissonance, far from being unpleasant, merely adds bite and tang to an otherwise colorless accompaniment—like two drops of Tabasco in a salad dressing.

But Rodgers' most effective trick is that of suddenly introducing an extraneous note—one that is foreign to the scale to which a given tune is written. Take, for example, the unexpected D-major in the third measure of "What's the Use of Wond'rin'?" from the second act of *Carousel*.

It relieves what otherwise would be an unadorned scale:

Or take this phrase from "A Cockeyed Optimist" (*South Pacific*):

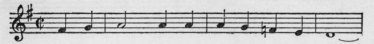

Anyone else would have written this, which would have been entirely commonplace:

One of the best examples is the opening of the "March of the Siamese Children" from *The King and I*—

—where that wholly unwarranted B-natural, coming out of left field, so to speak, creates an atmosphere of foreignness that is exactly what is needed. The classic example of the Rodgers Patented Wrong Note is the opening of "Oh, What a Beautiful Mornin'." He could have written it:

—which could have been written by any Viennese composer.

Or he could have written it thus:

—which would have anticipated the climax of the tune, and so spoiled it. What he did write, in a moment of pure inspiration, was:

—which makes the song the charming thing it is.

What luck for Hammerstein!

Some time ago I read an article in which Cole Porter, who is, after all, no mean composer in his own right, was quoted as saying, "I can spot one of Dick Rodgers' tunes anywhere. There's a sort of holiness about them." Someone else announced, in print, that Rodgers "has entered the realm of the folk art of America." Still another admirer announced that "they have a sadness about them." Those are all strong words with which to describe, incorrectly, the peculiar appeal of his music. It isn't holy, and it isn't folksy, and it isn't sad. But it is music made the way folk songs are made. He is a composer for the stage, and his music, consequently, is essentially vocal music. There is a conversational quality about it that makes it easy to sing. It lets the words through. It is music that was heard first in the composer's head, that was hummed or sung before it was harmonized. He is the exact counterpart of Hammerstein. Both say their say as directly as possible and as simply as possible. The trimmings may come later, but the tune itself, the lyric itself, is a simple thing. It is fundamental, but not holy. It is not sad, but it is serious. It is not folk song because it is not artless, but it has folk qualities. Stephen Foster, in another incarnation, might have written the lyrics and music of *Oklahoma!*

Starting from *Oklahoma!* by the way, their partnership has been distinguished by a consistent drive toward something that may become a new musico-dramatic form; something that is not "grand" opera, but is very definitely neither musical comedy nor operetta. Slight as its dramatic content is, *Oklahoma!* nevertheless *is* a drama, compared with the average musical comedy book and lyrics. *Carousel* is a completely successful attempt to translate a serious play to the musical stage—a compassionate story of the anguished love of a hopelessly inarticulate human being, a man who can express deep emotion only by violence.

Moss Hart is credited with giving the following advice to budding playwrights: "If you have a message, call Western Union." If he really said that, it is a somewhat cynical and curiously inconsistent dictum to come from a man who wrote a musical comedy extolling the virtues of psycho-analysis! However, if it were revised to read, "If you have a message, don't make it your whole story," there would be a certain amount of truth in it. *Allegro* suffered, I think, from its own earnestness. The idea, that of taking a man from birth to young middle-age, sounds like a good one. But the piece turned out to be a cavalcade rather than a play; and a cavalcade can hold an audience only if its separate episodes are exciting enough to make up for the lack of dramatic conflict. The message, reduced to its essentials, merely announced that cities and city people are a bad lot, and getting back to the soil is the way to save one's soul.

(Such is my recollection of what *Allegro* had to say. If I have done Mr. Hammerstein an injustice, if I am misquoting or oversimplifying, I can only apologize and say that I disagree with him anyhow.)

*South Pacific*, on the other hand, is a brilliant example of a play that delivers its message with complete success. The theme is, of course, that racial intolerance is an ugly and stupid thing; but the authors have not made the mistake of making it the star. They give us a beautiful and moving love story, with intolerance merely as the villain, who is defeated. In *The King and I*, the authors took a brave step. Not only did they have a fundamental theme —the struggle between freedom and tyranny—but they gave us a tragic story of a love that could never be avowed, a story of two people whose environments and training were such that they could never cross the chasm that yawned between them. Furthermore, the authors dared to end a musical play with a death scene. The complete triumph of *The King and I* is a tribute both to their skill and to their faith in the intelligence of the theatergoing public.

If the score of *Carousel* is the most tuneful that Rodgers ever wrote—as, in my opinion, it is—then *The King and I* must be counted as his best *score*, that is, the score that contributes the most to the dramatic development. There is a small group of outstanding "hit" songs, but the bulk of the score is devoted to carrying on the action. Hammerstein, too, has sacrificed his prospects for getting on the Hit Parade by writing lyrics, inseparable from the plot, such as "My Lord and Master," "It's a Puzzlement," "Shall I Tell You What I Think of You?" and "Western People Funny." The music for the ballet, "The Small House of Uncle Tom," is minimized to the point of being almost sound effects, with the result that it enhances, without interfering with the enchanting doings on stage. *The King and I* may or may not sell many record albums or pieces of sheet music; but it is magnificent theater.

Early in 1952 it transpired that Rodgers and Hammerstein were at work on a new piece—which is to say that

233

they were at the talking stage of the story, with dialogue, lyrics, and music yet to be set down. The two are notoriously averse to much advance publicity, and the bare announcement was all that they would permit at the moment. Indeed, when one intrepid reporter—meaning this correspondent—approached the office staff in the hope of seducing them into telling him the story, or failing that, at least the title, he was received with a decided lack of cordiality. One might have thought that he was inquiring after the Pope's telephone number. They are a loyal crew in that office!

In due time, however, the title and the other ingredients were assembled, rehearsed, and tried out on the road; and on the evening of Thursday, May 28, 1953, *Me and Juliet* opened at the Majestic Theatre in New York (*South Pacific* having courteously withdrawn for a brief road tour, after which it reopened at the Broadway Theatre).

*Me and Juliet* proved to be a cavalcade (an "original," not an adaptation) of life backstage in the theater, a show within a show, a chronicle of the fortunes of a theatrical company in a musical comedy, *Me and Juliet*, that has settled down for a run in a Broadway theater. It enlists the services of seventy-four actors, singers, and dancers, with a stage and electrical crew of about the same size. There are two love stories, one comic, the other melodramatic, in the telling of which we are taken all over the theater—backstage, facing an imaginary audience, onstage, facing a real one, the smoking room, the company manager's office, the alley, the bar across the street, the electricians' bridge—so many scenes, in fact, that they are not even listed in the program.

Many of the episodes in the piece are drawn from life—two lives, in fact: those of Rodgers and Hammerstein. The hero of *Me and Juliet,* for instance, is a youngster starting out in the theater as an assistant stage manager, just as Hammerstein did, thirty-six years ago. The opening night cast was headed by Bill Hayes, Isabel Bigley, and Joan Mc-Cracken. Jo Mielziner had designed the sets, Irene Sharaff had provided the costumes, and Robert Alton had staged the songs and dances. George Abbott had directed the book.

The reaction of the dramatic critics was a curious one, ranging from vehement disapproval to wholehearted embracement, with a middle-ground verdict that can be described only by my favorite adjective, ambivalent. There was nothing ambivalent, however, about Robert Coleman, of the *Mirror*:

Having set new high standards for musicals throughout the world, Richard Rodgers and Oscar Hammerstein dipped into the lower drawer of their desk for a song-and-dancer called *Me and Juliet* . . . a pedestrian musical. . . . George Abbott has staged the book for all it's worth . . . acceptable sets . . . fair-to-middling costumes . . . it isn't pleasant to tell you . . . that *Me and Juliet* is a mistake.

William Hawkins, of the *World-Telegram & Sun,* climbed the fence:

One of the most exciting things about Rodgers and Hammerstein . . . is that they never repeat themselves. In *Me and Juliet* they have copied nobody at all, and the resultant novelty is often a fascinating use of the theater . . . The action has so many places to go and so much to establish that it is a long time before anything reaches out and really "sends" you.

Brooks Atkinson, of the *Times* said yes and no:

When Mr. Rodgers and Mr. Hammerstein make up their minds what they are writing about, *Me and Juliet* . . . may turn out to be an enjoyable show . . . Mr. Rodgers has written one of his most melodious scores . . . Although the content of the story is romantic and attractive, the form is unwieldy and verbose . . . it would be hard to collect a more attractive cast . . . *Me and Juliet* looks better than a million dollars: it is gayer and more entrancing. . . . As the tired sages of show business invariably remark as though one phrase could solve everything: "It needs work."

Richard Watts, of the *Post*, turned thumbs down, up, and down:

There is no escaping the fact that Rodgers and Hammerstein are not at the top of their distinguished form in their new musical play. . . . It isn't a bore . . . lively, vigorous, and filled with the showmanlike craftsmanship of its makers . . . a number of attractive songs . . . lyrics are bright and intelligent . . . good-looking and ingeniously mounted . . . attractive singing actors. . . . There is a curious and surprising air of the commonplace hanging ominously over the evening.

The real hero of the occasion—in the eyes of Rodgers and Hammerstein at least—was undoubtedly John Mason Brown of the *Saturday Review*:

Mielziner conquers the usual physical limitations of the theatre. . . . Equally enchanting to the eye are Irene Sharaff's costumes. . . . Rodgers' music . . . is lively, fresh, and charming. . . . Hammerstein's lyrics are warmhearted, witty, and skilful. . . . George Abbott's direction has the expected drive. . . . Robert Alton's dances are spirited and original. . . . In the leading parts . . . all gifted and attractive. . . . An exceptionally entertaining and beautifully professional musical.

One reason, I think, for the half-reproachful mood of so many of the reviews of *Me and Juliet* is that the critics didn't read the first page of their programs carefully enough. Every one of the previous stage pieces by Rodgers and Hamin the *New York Times*, was typical:

*Victory at Sea* . . . is a documentary film of rare power and poetry. With a superlative score by Richard Rodgers, the series . . . is not alone history but a drama told with moving simplicity and restrained majesty. . . . Hardly enough can be said for the score of Mr. Rodgers. . . . Especially in the portions accompanying scenes of the sea and the tension of battle, his work has a compelling beauty and vigor that adds incalculably to the emotional intensity of the series.

In the *World-Telegram and Sun*, Harriet van Horne had this to say:

Another distinguishing feature of *Victory at Sea* is the original score by Richard Rodgers. Not being a music critic, I lack tongue to praise it. I only know that it's music one feels. And it's music that's exactly right for each scene.

The other critics were equally enthusiastic, including the London critics when the BBC televised the series in England.

While Hammerstein had no direct connection with *Victory at Sea*, nevertheless I can't help thinking that, in a way, he had a share in its creation. The musical plays upon which he and Rodgers had worked together—*Carousel, South Pacific, The King and I*—had had moments that called for music that was something more than tuneful, that had emotional depth and drama as well. Rodgers had risen to the challenge; *Victory at Sea* found him ready.

Incidentally, the score is not all drama and emotion. Two popular pieces have already emerged from it: the "Guadalcanal March," upon which the bandmasters have already laid gleeful hands, and the tango that all of us now know as "No Other Love," from *Me and Juliet*.

# Index

# Index

# Index

# Index

# Index

# Index